DEDICATION

To Sarah,
You captured my heart and
filled my quiver with arrows.

CONTENTS

ACKNOWLEDGMENTS

I thank our kids for their grace and endless supply of content, our extended family for pouring into them, Dan Branch for noticing a talent and encouraging it, my newspaper column readers for giving me a reason to hone my craft, Mom for making me write all those thank you notes, Dad for writing me all those poems and Susie Allen for giving me a deadline.

INTRODUCTION: STARTING FIVE

When I tell people we have five children, they fumble to fill the silence.

"Wow! You have your own basketball team!"

When we pull up to a party and the clowns pour out of the van, questions follow.

"Did you come from a large family?"

"Are you Catholic or Mormon?"

"Are they all yours?"

"Possibly," I respond. "Let's see how they act."

Life happened fast. Eighteen months after our wedding day, Sarah was pregnant with our first son. Two more sons came in the next five years.

Shortly before our third son arrived, we had a decision to make: Cut our losses and wait for daughters-in-law and granddaughters, or roll the dice for a princess.

"Are we tying your tubes today, ma'am?" a delivery nurse asked.

Sarah and I glanced at each other.

"I don't think so," she said feeling lucky, I suppose. A year went by, and we fell pregnant again. We were, in fact, gambling for a girl. Nine months later...

Jackpot! We got her!!!

Along with her twin brother.

For those keeping score at home, that's four boys and a girl. In six and a half years, Sarah plus Kevin made seven.

When our county judge heard the news, he advised, "Son, Sarah needs to start sleeping with two feet in one sock."

Our oldest son, six at the time, showed wisdom beyond his years when we told him about the twins.

"Aww, man," he said. "That's gonna be a lot of work."

While we cleaned out our house to make room for the twins, I happened upon a book in a stack destined for a resale shop. It was in near-mint condition.

The title? *Taking Control of Your Fertility*

"Oh, there it is," I thought, with a touch of nonchalance.

If we just had mastered that content, how much more orderly would life be? How many more manners would be taught? How many more college accounts would be fully funded?

All true, but also this: How much less fun and funny?

Here comes the fun, the funny and the lessons learned while starting five kids into the game of life.

Are you ready? Have you washed your hands?

Yes, I know you're going to use a fork! You still need to wash your hands!!!

1 THE FIVE YEAR RULE

You probably know the five second rule. If food drops on the floor, you have five seconds to retrieve and consume it before it officially becomes unsanitary.

When one of our sons was eight, he dropped a chip on the floor. A few seconds later he looked around and slowly picked it up. He popped it into his mouth and announced to his repulsed siblings, "Five year rule!"

That's how things sometimes go in our super-sized family; we have to make our own rules.

As a four-year-old, the same son who coined the five year rule had explained why a chore assignment wouldn't work for him.

"I can't clean the kitchen. I'm sick! I don't want to spread my germs!" He has such a big heart.

Raising five kids can certainly make five years feel like five seconds.

You turn around, and they're off to kinder. You turn around again, and they're producing body odor. You turn around once more, and they're taking driver's ed.

Before you know it, they're on their own, and you're left holding a bag of baby teeth. I plan to string those teeth into a necklace for Sarah when the last two leave home.

Those teeth will surely have a few cavities in them thanks to the sticky years, that span of time when everything is sticky.

Gummy bears dance on teeth, peanut butter covers fingers, watermelon juice coats floors, and Chik-fil-a© Polynesian Sauce lines auto interiors.

But here's the irony: The sticky years don't stick around for long. Long days, short years, as they say.

Sarah and I try to savor the sticky years at the behest of reminiscing empty nesters. We try to remember what's important, those things that will actually matter in a hundred years.

And we try to remember the basics, like underwear, without getting our panties in a wad.

"Dad, what's the point of underwear?" one of our sons asked once. He was convinced it was superfluous, like a napkin when you have a shirt sleeve or the back of your hand.

It's no small wonder any of our kids actually has underwear on - and that it's not a pair of shorts, or a swimsuit.

It's also no small wonder we ever get subject and a verb to agree, or that all 147 meals get made - and cleaned up - each week, or that all 245 articles of clothing get washed - and put away - each week.

At one time I told people there's not much difference between having two kids and having five, that at some point economies of scale kick in. I lied.

Comedian Jim Gaffigan, also a father of five, says having a bunch of kids feels like you're drowning in a river - and then someone hands you a baby.

I decided long ago I'm not in control here; God is. And he always provides...for a family of four.

Or maybe he just agrees with Ben Franklin: "If you want something done, ask a busy person."

Not that we're actually getting a lot done. Kids are issued a pillow, a blanket and sometimes a towel. They more or less figure it out from there.

"Live in the day; measure in the decade," author Morgan Snyder says.

My good friend, Matt Murphy, reminds me there are many right ways to raise kids - and only a few wrong ones. I've repented from the wrong ones but only after adding a few to the list.

It's never too late to pick up the pieces, I try to remember. Today's love covers over a multitude of yesterday's sins.

Plus, as we often hear from parents who moved their children across the country in the middle of middle school, kids are resilient.

How else would they be able to put on the same pair of underwear after a bath as they had on before it?

2 A KID'S EYE VIEW

A great joy of fatherhood is hearing how the little people process life. As I tucked our four-year-old princess into bed one night, I asked her, "What are you going to dream about?"

"Just you," she whispered softly in my ear. I kissed her goodnight, levitated to my computer and pre-ordered a pink 2026 BMW convertible. Done. Her brothers can ride bikes.

Once, when she was ready to leave for a party, she bargained, "If you get dressed fast, I'll give you some gum and a new phone!" She knows technology unlocks my heart.

Her twin brother could have picked out the phone. As a four-year-old, he rounded the corner one day with my smartphone announcing with sass: "I know your password. You better change it." He was four!

While I was waiting for an email, my kids became fully native to the digital landscape.

When our third son, six at the time, came with me to work one day, he asked if he could call his mom from my office phone.

"Sure," I said, "but you'll need to dial nine first." He stared at me blankly. After repeating myself three times, he finally asked, "Do you mean 'push' nine?"

Yes, push nine.

On a spring break trip to a cabin in the woods, an eight-year-old tried unsuccessfully to check sports scores on my phone. Exasperated, he suffered, "Why don't they have Internet? I mean, they have lights!"

Another time, after Sarah got back from a shopping trip, she asked him, "Did you miss me?"

His honest reply: "No, but I missed your phone."

This kid rarely misses his sports highlights or his basketball shots. I once asked him why you get two points for a field goal in basketball.

"Because the ball goes through both the rim and the net," he reasoned. Not bad.

His little brother is also still learning how basketball scoring works.

"Hey Dad, Lebron James scored nine and a half points last night," he informed me one morning.

"How did he get that half point?" I asked curiously.

"He made a free throw," he explained matter-of-factly.

Speaking of foul shots, the brothers' little sister shoots free throws granny-style, or, as she describes it, "sumo style."

As in most families with a lot of boys, sports are a very serious business. When a six-year-old and I were playing catch in the yard, he announced, "Here comes the last out of the World Serious!"

We haven't mastered other sports terminology.

"Dad?" our daughter asked with fielder's glove in hand. "Will you throw me some *underground* balls?" She must not have been ready for pop-ups.

A three-year-old son once handed me three tennis balls and asked, "Will you *jiggle* these?"

It's not just sports terms we butcher. Any vocabulary can be a crap shoot in our house.

On hot summer days, we try not to forget our "sunscream." We try not to contract "chicken pops" from kids at school. Sometimes we watch movies on "Nexflips." If you want to know the price of something at the store, just scan its "zebra name tag."

Our little girl loves music. She once asked her twin brother, "How 'bout you dance and I sing?" Lyrics are not yet her forte.

"How much is that doggie in the rainbow?"

"From the mountains to the *cherries*, to the oceans white with foam…"

"…it's our problem-free, *it means a lot to me*, Hakuna Matata!"

At times she plays around on the keyboard. I asked her once if she'd like to take piano lessons.

"No, thanks," she answered. "I like improvising."

Sarah and I try to teach the kids what matters most in life. It doesn't always click.

Here's a six-year-old's translation of Proverbs 3:5: "Trust in the Lord with all your heart. *Lean back* on your own understanding."

Here's an eight-year-old's definition of gratitude: great attitude.

When I asked a brother what verse he learned in Bible class, he said, "Treat the Lord the way you want to be treated."

Before dinner one night, I asked for someone to complete this sentence: "The family that prays together…."

Expecting "stays together," all I got was "eats together." The family that prays together, eats together?!? Heathens and gluttons, all of them! Their god is in their stomachs!

We don't always get the details – or the big picture. After I told our little girl we always need to be ready for Jesus' return, she asked, "Will he want to see our rooms?"

And then there was the time shortly after Halloween when she asked me, "What do you want to be for Thanksgiving?"

A pilgrim, dear, a pilgrim, wandering through the wild wilderness called fatherhood.

3 FRONTAL LOBE DEVELOPMENT

A baby blue sign hung in our home for many years: "Thank Heaven for Little Boys."

Homes with four little girls don't operate like ours. A father there doesn't shuffle in darkness to the bathroom in the middle of the night only to descend onto cold, wet porcelain. Girls simply don't leave toilet seats up.

"What's it like having four brothers?" a friend asked our daughter once.

"Tiring," she said with a sigh.

Sarah reminds me often how undeveloped a boy's frontal lobe is – you know, the part of the brain used for basic decision-making. The part that makes gravity, germs and other pesky forces of nature non-negotiable.

In a family of boys, I hear a lot of "O-O-O-O'Reilly's…Private Parts" (instead of "…Auto Parts"), "Who wants to dogpile?" and "Will you please tackle me?"

Two-hand touch football is as foreign a concept as daily bathing or washing hands after wiping.

One time, our oldest son pounced on his little brother who was about two at the time. It was rough, physical contact. I feared for the toddler's health.

But the toddler did not cry, at least not immediately. Only

after I removed his big brother from on top of him did he cry hysterically. I had stolen his playmate!

Bodily functions consume plenty of air in our house. When I asked a five-year-old, "Who passed gas?" he blamed it on the TV actors. Our TV is smart, but not that smart.

"Hey, Dad," another son announced once. "Did you know you can burn 63 calories just by farting?"

For as inaccurate as boys can be at the toilet, they are remarkably precise with a gun, if not with the truth.

"I shot a dove with my BB gun, but he flew away," one reported dubiously.

Other weapons can be just as deadly in the right small hands.

"I saw three deer and killed them all with my pocket knife," a five-year-old told me once.

If worms lure fish, water baits boys. The longer you stay near water, the more likely boys will get wet. It's a natural law.

Temperature and attire make no difference. Neither do current speed or depth. It is simply a matter of time, despite maternal pleadings to stay dry.

One year our church had Easter service on the town square. Their Easter best didn't stop the Thompson boys from immersing in the town fountain.

Boy moms have a vernacular all their own. They have a knack for redirecting activity without squelching fun. For example, "You are welcome to do that...outside."

Other times they direct without question: "You MUST wear shoes!"

Mumbling to themselves is no sign of mental instability.

"Just when I think it can't get any louder..." I heard Sarah say once.

Boy moms simply can't stop all supernatural feats of exploration. During a birthday party in our backyard, I heard a kid say, "Hey, look! That baby just climbed over that fence."

Mothers do their best to cultivate character and culture, sometimes without effect. A Bible class teacher once asked our four-year-old son for a song suggestion.

"Tonight's Gonna Be A Good Night!" he answered.

Thank you, Black Eyed Peas. May you always be eaten.

The simplicity of boys is certainly refreshing.

One Christmas, the only present my oldest son wanted was a mouthpiece, the kind football players, boxers and boys with three brothers use to protect their teeth. They're a buck fifty at Walmart.

Hmmm. Cheap and useful. Maybe those frontal lobes aren't so undeveloped after all.

4 AN OLFACTORY QUANDARY

With so many boys in a family, smells come with the territory.

I'm still not a smells guy. If there's any question whether a piece of clothing is dirty or clean, it's dirty. I don't smell it.

So, when the need arose to investigate a foul smell in the house, I didn't volunteer cheerfully.

The smell appeared to descend from the bedroom of my oldest sons, ages ten and seven at the time. When they denied the root resided in their room - a wet swimsuit mildewing or an apple core molding - I didn't believe them.

Donning an industrial grade dust mask, I made a timid inspection of the upstairs bedroom only to concur with the boys: the culprit was not in their room.

Next stop: laundry room.

With four growing boys, the laundry plays host to many ogre-worthy odors. A kindergartener once obediently wiped up his spilled milk, and then tossed the milk-soaked rag *behind* the washing machine.

This time, however, a weak-stomached inspection of the laundry room turned up empty.

The process of (odor) elimination finally took me to the garage. Surely a bottle of putrid deer repellent had spilled, the rotten egg substance that keeps Bambi from stopping to smell – and eat – the roses.

Still, nothing conclusive! As I stood in the hallway - equidistant from the boys' bedroom, the laundry room and the garage - I resigned to call an expert. There must be a dead squirrel in the attic.

Then, an epiphany.

The hallway where I stood has five hooks on wall, one for every child's backpack. My squinched nose began its investigation of the packs, including a third grade boy's.

Third grade is a great time for most kids. They've had a few years to get comfortable with school. Pre-adolescent hormones haven't started pulsating. A boy might think a girl is cute but she's not going to invite him to a party. Deodorant remains conveniently optional.

In third grade, a kid is both old enough to buy an extra chocolate milk for the road and still young enough to completely forget about it over a three-day weekend.

As I picked up this kid's backpack, a thick liquid dripped on my leg. I hoped it was from the water bottle kids are required to keep at their desks nowadays. It wasn't.

I proceeded to examine the backpack's 17 different compartments. Finally, at the bottom of the center-left-middle-vertical-zippered pocket, I saw - and smelled - the source of our discomfort.

A curdled substance seeped from a soft-sided lunch box. Inside, secretions oozed from a breach in a bloated, lukewarm milk carton.

Got milk? Yes. And yogurt and cottage cheese and pudding and whipping cream.

I immediately called the principal. Forget metal detectors at school entrances. I want milk detectors at the exits!

5 HAPPY BIRTHDAY, LINCHPIN!

One year, our third son's birthday celebration lasted nearly a month.

Since it was his fourth birthday, and since his birthday is in July, and since fireworks explode on July 4th, he was convinced he shared a birthday with the United States of America.

His older brothers tried to tell him his birthday immutably falls on July 24. He would have none of it.

He has always been a tough sell. One time, after he had told a lie, I explained that he must always tell the truth.

"But I'm not Jesus!" he argued.

Honesty is not his best policy.

Another time, he took a chocolate chip cookie from the kitchen without asking.

Me: "Son, what's behind your back?"

Son: "Mom told me I could have one."

Me, to his mother in another room: "Mom, did you say Cooper could have a cookie?"

Mom: "No."

He slowly handed me the contraband: "I'll just have one tomorrow."

I admire his confidence in the father's mercy.

During a family devotional, I invited the kids to share a time they were selfish and only thought about themselves.

When he struggled to grasp the concept, I suggested the time when he stole a classmate's ice cream ticket.

He clarified, "I wasn't thinking about myself. I was thinking about ice cream!"

I call this son "Linchpin." He has two older siblings and two younger siblings. He's the quintessential middle child. He gets it from both ends.

No wonder he thinks you get "punched" if you're not wearing green on St. Patrick's Day.

If Linchpin is well, the family system is usually stable, too. Or, as Sarah says, if the linchpin is out, the bomb has gone off.

Remarkably, he's our most fun-loving, extroverted soul. He had a troop of high school girls cheering his bunny hops at a pizza parlor one time. As a three-year-old he wore a Davy Crockett-style coonskin cap to church one Sunday.

If I can't find him at a public event, I look toward the stage. He's usually there.

We scheduled one of his birthday parties to piggyback on a YMCA-sponsored "Flick & Float" at the city pool.

We didn't tell him all the people weren't there for him, mostly because they weren't strangers. They were just friends he'd not yet met, much like Hank, the "hybrid" puppy our family adopted the next day.

He thought the dog was a birthday gift just for him. That's fine with me. The more children responsible for my backyard sanitation, the better.

Linchpin is certainly an expert in all things fecal. As I stuffed a pair of dress slacks into a dry cleaning bag, he asked, "Why did you put those in there?"

I explained that's where I put them when they get dirty.

"You mean when you get tee-tee and poo-poo on them?"

Sure, son, if that helps.

Happy Birthday, Linchpin! May your trousers always be dry. And may you always find a cleaners to take them to when they're not.

6 A FINE(D) CANINE

Now about Hank, the family cow dog. He is a chocolate lab mutt. Pardon me. He's a mix, not a mutt. "Mutt" is now insensitive and politically incorrect. Somehow, it's still okay to multiply a girl dog's age by seven.

As a puppy, Hank observed only one rule when it came to chewing: Only chew things of value. Library books, baseball gloves, ladies dress shoes. New toys, yard tools, antique furniture. All equally delicious.

A rubber tire scrap? Not interested.

We lost Hank once. After Sarah and I had left the kids with a sitter for the evening, we returned and he was gone, lost.

The next morning, the kids had no clue. I prepared to follow the same rescue steps I had used a month prior when New Year's fireworks spooked him over the fence and down to the corner store.

Then, our kindergartener went to retrieve his backpack from the car. Moments later, he busted back through the front door with his backpack, a canine and some news, "Hank was in the car!"

Hank, the rescue dog, was rescued again but not before completely chewing through a seat belt.

Another time, when Hank decided to take a stroll down the

street, the pound came calling.

Animal Control Officer (ACO): "Mr. Thompson? This is animal services. Do you own a dog named 'Hank'?"

Me: "Yes."

ACO: "Could you have recently failed to keep him under proper restraint and permitted him to be at large away from your premises?"

Me: "Possibly."

ACO: "Do you know if Hank has a license?"

Me (laughing): "A license?"

ACO: "Yes, a license. I don't see one here in our records."

According to the officer, a city ordinance requires every dog to have a license. They're four dollars each. I had no idea. Hank had no idea either.

"Ruff! Ruff!" he exclaimed. "There was no sign!"

The city ordinance reminded me of Ronald Reagan:

"Government's view of the economy can be summed up in a few short phrases: If it moves, tax it. If it keeps moving, regulate it. And if it stops moving, subsidize it."

Hank was moving, so I had to pay the tax.

I'm sure there are public health and safety reasons for authorities to know what pets occupy our neighborhoods. But taxing a man's dog seems un-American, definitely un-Texan.

Together with the fees I paid the county shelter for the right to rescue Hank, and the hundreds of dollars in veterinary bills since then, I must now fork over four bones for a pet license?!? No wonder the sorry dog thinks he deserves table scraps - no, table food!

After exercising three weeks of civil disobedience, an envelope from the city arrived. Inside was a green carbon copy of a Code Enforcement citation. It read like a traffic ticket.

Violator: Thompson

Color: Tan

Year / Model: "Hank"

Make: Lab / X (X is for mix)

Violation: 6605 - Unlicensed Dog

The summons ordered me to appear in municipal court.

I modified my civil disobedience plan and decided to get Hank a license. He would sniff, chew and mark his territory above reproach.

As I entered the animal control office, an orange feline greeted me. His fur was shaved to look like a lion.

"Are cats licensed, too?" I inquired, only half serious and with irritation in my voice.

"Yes. And if you have more than four cats or dogs, you'll need a permit. They are $100 a year."

I quit asking questions. I feared a syllable tax.

The officer briefed me on a dog license, and I wrote a $4.00 check to legalize Hank.

As I stepped toward the door, I could tell the officer's wheels were turning.

"So, do you have a cat?" he asked.

Pumpkin is technically not mine. He belongs to the person who left him at the restaurant where he rubbed his soft kitten fur against my five-year-old son's leg.

Fearing the syllable tax, I responded simply to the officer, "Yes." My eyes never left the floor.

Four more dollars later, I headed to municipal court ready to waive all my new pet licenses in front of the judge and jury. All Hank's charges would soon be dropped.

Not so fast, buddy.

According to the city attorney, Hank's file had already wandered too far. I owed both a fine and court costs. Hank did have an option, the attorney told me: deferment.

If Hank exhibits good behavior for ninety days, the citation would stay off my record. My record?!? What about his?!?

Dumbfounded, I asked the judge if community service were an option. Hank would do well at a nursing home or a pre-school. He wouldn't hurt a flea, I told the judge, unless it was on his belly.

With a smirk, the judge passed me to the clerk. The clerk passed me to the cashier who passed me back my debit card after charging it for more than I ever thought I'd spend on that sorry dog.

7 ROAD TRIP PROFUNDITIES

Fourteen hours crammed in a car with 2 parents and 5 kids under 10 on a road trip across the south. What's there to learn?

Plenty, including the obvious, "Don't do this again!" Here's more:

1. There are many nice cars on the road. You're not in one of them.

2. There are clean restrooms out there. You will not find them.

3. Your neighbor will offend you. My neighbor said my packed vehicle looked a little like Clark Griswold's of Vacation movie fame. I was offended. The nerve of him. My vehicle looked A LOT like Clark Griswold's!

4. Your three-year-old will know if you deposit anything sweet into your mouth. He was on the back row next to the window watching a video.

How could he possibly have seen, much less identified, my subtle nose scratch that may or may not have included the placement of candy in my mouth?

"I want some M&M's!" Me, too. Me, too. Me, too. Me, too.

5. Your children don't know their landforms. In rural Louisiana, I asked my oldest son what we were traveling through. I expected "swamp" or "bayou" or "marsh." Instead

he guessed, "Redneck?" Thank you, Duck Dynasty.

6. Mothers of boys are quite poetic. As we loaded back up from a stop, my wife invited her four sons to "speak now or forever hold your pee."

7. Brothers will go to extreme lengths to annoy their siblings. "Mom! He won't wipe his boogers! They're running down his face!"

8. Your wife will ridicule your attempts at modern entertainment technology.

Too cheap for a professional mobile entertainment system, I forked over $200 for two Velcro-strapped video screens, a power inverter and an 8 foot extension cord - the extension cord because I'm too cheap to fix the cigarette lighter in the front – only the one in the back works.

By 11:00 p.m. on the eve of our trip, I had cords crisscrossing our SUV's interior, but I had a video system that worked. I even had the audio piped through the vehicle speakers - okay, through the left speakers; the right side quit about a year ago.

Full of pride, I invited Sarah to see the masterpiece. It held the promise of hours of roadway peace.

"It looks like a rolling Radio Shack," she said. "Someone could get hung in there."

That's it. I'm done! Back to books, "I spy" and old-fashioned imagination.

The curse of modern mobile media systems is they create the expectation that long distance travel is easier than it used to be.

It isn't. It's still a long, hard slog through bayous, brothers and boogers.

8 A FAMILY FISH TALE

The best thing about travelling to see family is you get to see your loved ones in their elements.

For instance, your camo-clad, bass boat-owning brother-in-law fishing on a dammed up piece of the Tennessee River.

"That's why you never give up!!!" Jeremy exclaimed.

His motivating statement was not referring to a big catch. He and his fishing buddy, Dan, had just freed his stuck lure after about ten minutes of trying.

The process included the use of a "plug knocker," a weighted tool designed to retrieve lines trapped underwater.

"Plug knocker" wasn't the only vernacular I learned on Lake Chickamauga ('mauga for short). There was also "Alabama Rig," a massive, shiny, multi-hook lure that could double as mobile home chandelier.

It looked like someone had dropped a decent-sized magnet into a kitchen junk drawer.

The rig dangled and sparkled and spun as it hung on the line. In the water, it looked like a small school of fish.

Alabama Rigs are for experienced anglers like Jeremy and Dan.

As a novice, I used a spinner reel with something called a rattletrap.

"It took my kids a whole year to learn how to cast the Alabama," Jeremy told me.

Solid planning is a key part of the routine. During our pre-dawn drive to Chattanooga, I was in the back seat trying to catch some zzz's. Jeremy and Dan strategized up front.

"Let's start at Turkey Foot and catch three or four to get our confidence up," Jeremy said. He was completely serious.

I have always considered fishing a game of chance: There are fish in a body of water like there are aces in a deck of cards. You drop your line, and, depending on your luck, you may be a winner.

My sister married into a family where such thinking is illogical at best and sacrilege at worst.

To her in-laws, fishing involves as much skill as any other sport, and it carries the same hope of glory.

"On any given cast, you could catch the state record," Jeremy informed me with the straightest of faces. "That's why we come here."

His nod to fishing immortality came midway through our nine uninterrupted hours on the water.

As with any sport, competition is part of the equation. Stealing a fisherman's favorite spot on the lake is like sitting in Grandma's pew at church.

"That guy is going straight for the sand bar! Go!" Jeremy yelled to Dan who happened to be closest to the throttle. "Cut him off!!!"

Judging by the intensity of the moment, you would think Lake Chickamauga was only a few acres across.

It is actually fifty-seven square miles. It was created decades ago by the Tennessee Valley Authority.

Intensity is how we caught eighteen largemouth bass on a cold and rainy day in late December. My rattletrap accounted for one of them.

We threw all the fish back. For serious fishermen, it's not always about the destination. It's mostly about the journey.

Besides, we didn't actually need the fish as proof of our success. Who wouldn't take a fisherman's word for it?

9 TO THE MOUNTAINS AND BACK

I love to ski. I love to ski so much I'll ride twelve hours in a packed 7-passenger SUV. I'll ride those twelve hours in that packed SUV even if one of the six other passengers has the flu. I'll take my chances. I love to ski.

It takes this kind of perseverance to get two adults and five kids – all under twelve, one under the weather – to northern New Mexico, a place not easily accessible from south Texas.

Route options: (A) Drive west, then north and see cartoon aliens in Roswell, NM, or (B) Drive north, then west and smell Lubbock. I couldn't decide so we did both, one going and one coming. It really broke up the monotony.

Eating on the road is about as appetizing as eating off the road. Cheeseburgers, chicken fingers, repeat.

I never complained on a fast food chain's web site until we visited a Dairy Queen in rural west Texas. I've seen cleaner port-a-johns. My wife used the experience to teach the kids about the value of marketplace competition. Trust me, it was an anti-trust message for the ages.

Sleeping on the road is no dream either. Thank you, oil & gas industry, for the thrill of paying $275 for a single room at a Fairfield Inn in the middle of nowhere.

With one room for seven humans, we needed our four-year-old son to share a pull-out sofa with his six-year-old brother.

He vehemently refused.

"He's wearing panties!" he said. They were really just briefs.

Around midnight I retrieved a pillow from the car. A rough-looking roughneck startled me as I entered the elevator. I'm not sure what was on his mind, but it wasn't pillows.

That wasn't the only scary moment of the trip. I mistakenly trusted a smartphone map for my route through the mountains.

The route included a pass up snowy County Road 18 through a nearly-deserted Mora, New Mexico, right about dusk.

I've never felt more like a character in a horror movie.

We stopped beside a mountain stream to let the boys relieve themselves. In midstream, two men in an early 80s Chevy pickup drove past. About thirty seconds later they returned.

"These guys are up to no good," I thought.

They parked and got out.

"Hey, buddy, you got five dollars for gas?" one of them asked.

I needed to parse my answer.

A clear "yes" would open up my wallet to thievery. A "no" would be a clear lie from a Texas-plated vehicle full of kids and gear.

Murderers don't like liars, I reminded myself.

"I buy all my gas with a debit card," I responded.

The locals were perplexed but content with my answer.

Strangely, they drove off in a different direction than they were heading in originally. The snow angels surrounding us must have directed them that way.

After three days of learning to ski, the way home through the Texas Panhandle was also eventful. A four-year-old boy threw up on his eleven-year-old brother.

An eight-year-old asked "Who peed in their pants?" when we drove past cattle feed yards. This is the same kid who saw me in my long johns and asked, "Skinny jeans?"

Seven people endured another night in an overpriced motel room built for four.

While we loved our three days on the slopes, we'll probably

best remember our four days on the road!

10 BOAT RIDES HEADLINE
STAY-CATION

Stay-cation. I first heard the term during the summer of 2008 when gas prices jumped to four dollars a gallon.

I remember that summer well because I had just traded a Volkswagen for a 2003 Chevrolet Suburban, MPG: 14.

The term gained strength through the recession of 2009. It was perhaps more utilized in San Antonio because of our nearby tourist attractions (Six Flags, SeaWorld, The Alamo, etc.). A staycation in Shreveport is still probably known as a family budget cut.

After the recession, stay-cations were largely shelved. But when Sarah suggested I burn a few vacation days before school started back, I resurrected the stay-cation and priced out the usual suspects.

For a family of seven, one day at Six Flags would cost about $400; a day at SeaWorld, $500. And that's just for parking, discounted admission and one bucket of fried food.

Throw in a few rigged games, some stuffed souvenirs and a $25 refillable drink cup, a two-day escapade gets you well into the four-figures.

However, Six Flags' nightly fireworks display only costs the price of a family meal at the Mexican restaurant across the interstate. That's not being cheap. That's being innovative.

After thinking outside the tourism box, I called a local marina. They offered a pretty new 8-seat ski boat with all the accessories for about half the cost of a day at SeaWorld.

With positive attitudes, fishing bait and half a shelf of consumer packaged goods, we set sail. None of the above lasted long.

The positive attitudes fell in with our twelve-year-old son when he got thrown hard from the tube.

I didn't understand. He *asked* to be thrown hard from the tube. It's hard to want what we get when we get what we want!

Then, our ten-year-old son secretly tossed the bait overboard one minnow at a time. His sensitive heart couldn't stand to watch them get impaled by his eight-year-old brother with catfishing hooks.

All along, the store-bought snacks settled into stomachs like Jonah in the whale. The turkey sandwiches went untouched.

I couldn't stop them. What leverage does a parent have on a boat in the middle of a body of water?

As the boat rental time ran out, kids were still wanting tube rides. They still wanted to fish. And they wanted yet another plastic-wrapped cupcake.

We left the marina with plans to return and with our eyes set on a second staycation boat ride: a dinner cruise on the San Antonio Riverwalk.

In a plea for good behavior, Sarah explained to the kids that some couples would be on date nights.

I explained that "facilities" meant bathrooms, that there weren't any on the boat and that going off the side was not an option.

The kids minded their manners well. They stayed in their seats. They tried what was on their plates. They survived without lemonade. They even listened to the tour guide talk about things older than their dad.

Evidently, someone is listening during those broken-record family dinners at home, the ones where it feels like we're doing it all, again, for the first time.

Or maybe they just believed me when I said the annual dredging of the Riverwalk turns up jewelry, cell phones, patio chairs and misbehaving children.

How's that for leverage in the middle of a body of water?

11 MEMORIES OF SUMMER

Summer: blessing to educators and bane to homemakers.

With its long days and warm temperatures, summer arguably makes more memories than all the other seasons combined.

Nothing spells "summer" like VBS (Vacation Bible School).

Before the days of VBS-in-a-box - complete with soundtracks and t-shirts - I listened to a plump preacher conduct "sword drills" in a stuffy auditorium.

John 7:37? I got it! "Let anyone who is thirsty come to me and drink."

And drink we did on those humid middle Tennessee summer mornings.

McDonald's orange drink flowed freely from its famous yellow cooler.

Today, we don't live far from Six Flags' "Fiesta Texas" theme park in San Antonio.

For years, one of our sons called it "VBS-ta Texas." He begged us to go. He really wanted to learn how God stays with us through the ups and downs of life.

Back in Tennessee, my mother always looked hard for ways to keep us busy in the summer.

A friend once invited us to a private swimming pool tucked in the trees of a manicured south Nashville neighborhood.

Mom's car was in the shop that day, so we had to take Dad's extra work truck, a 1976 Ford dually. No AC, no power steering, no power brakes, no fun.

The flatbed's wooden sides barricaded the indiscriminately dumped trash Dad periodically cleared from behind shopping centers.

Mom wrestled the beast to the pool. I'm certain our arrival caused the cosmopolitans to rethink their commitment to diversity. I didn't notice. I simply swam up a huge appetite.

At that poolside snack bar, I discovered that nothing satisfies post-swimming hunger like a sandwich, an ice cream sandwich.

In Texas, my kids will learn some things at the pool this summer, too.

Someone will teach my preschooler that the legendary pool game is called 'Marco Polo,' not Marco "Pillow." It's not going to be me.

For several summers in the mid-1980s, Mom borrowed an Apple II computer from the elementary school where she taught.

Since our family rarely roughed it beyond a Motel 6, Oregon Trail became my gateway to the frontier.

An educational computer game, Oregon Trail taught children the realities of 19th century pioneer life. It mainly taught me worst-case scenarios:

1. A wheel could come off your wagon.

2. Your kids could starve because you can't hunt worth a darn.

3. Your wife may drown while fording a river.

4. You could die of dysentery.

Crap.

Oregon Trail prepared me for our annual church camp near the tallest North American waterfall south of Niagara: Fall Creek Falls in east Tennessee. The falls were fatal to fall over but a rush to swim under.

The waterfall wasn't the only water that washed over me at that camp.

One year I was baptized after a campfire devotional on the

last night of camp. A great cloud of witnesses surrounded the swimming hole.

Thirty minutes later I was filling water balloons in preparation for a midnight raid of a rival cabin.

Salvation is instant; sanctification takes time.

It was a night for obeying Jesus, including his instructions in Matthew 18: "Unless you change and become like little children, you shall never enter the kingdom of heaven."

12 A NEW FAMILY MOTTO

The little people can be so absent-minded. In a house full of them, I am constantly amazed at how frequently things shift.

It's as if inanimate objects grow legs and wheels and wings and propellers. I thought it would get better with time. It hasn't.

Kids are like tornadoes. They pick up random items, spin around a bunch of times, and spit out whatever they sucked up wherever they touch down.

I once found a half-eaten granola bar in my truck's glove compartment. Another time I found peanut butter on a doorknob two rooms away from the kitchen.

The radioactive fluorescent goop inside glow sticks has ruined multiple pieces of wood furniture when the sticks weren't returned to their proper place, preferably the trash.

"Everything has a place," I explain to little eyes that look straight through me to the next spot their owner can discard something that doesn't belong there.

An anatomical law is at play here: As soon as a child's mind moves to its next thought, his or her hand muscles immediately atrophy and release whatever was in their grasp.

I used to say, "Wash your hands." Now I'm forced to include, "and put the hand towel back on the rack when you're done!"

Otherwise it ends up on the floor, or in the bathtub, or tied around the cat's neck.

Like most kids, ours have trouble turning off lights when they leave a room. Our electric bill has hit an all-time high.

Fortunately, what they give away in electricity, they make up for in water. I rarely find a toilet that's been flushed.

I recently decided it was time to establish a new household motto. With credit to the state parks department, here it is: "Leave no trace."

It took some time to explain to the kids that our new family motto could co-exist with an old one, "Make your mark." It's a paradox, I said.

The new motto worked exactly one time:

A child entered the powder room, closed the door, did his business and then exited.

When the paternal park ranger entered the powder room, he found the soap dispenser upright on the sink top, not hanging from a curtain rod.

He found all clean toilet paper properly enrolled on the spool, not spread in seventeen separate sheets across the floor.

And he found the hand towel hanging on its hook, not submerged in six inches of bubbles in the wash basin.

Save the odor, the child had successfully left no trace! I was ecstatic. I just knew the maternal calls for paid housekeeping help would dissipate like a fresh squeeze of Febreze!

I also knew there needed to be some teeth in the novel domestic policy. Unfortunately, executing consequences has never been my parenting forte.

I would deduct fines from their allowances if I gave allowances out with any regularity. I would make kids miss the big game if I didn't want to watch it myself.

If I had received an allowance for every chore chart I've constructed in the last fifteen years, I could order maid service for the next fifteen.

Many years ago, I downloaded a smartphone app called Chore Monster. It was designed to help parents help kids remember their chores. I dutifully entered all the kids and all their chores.

Years later, Chore Monster keeps emailing me that my kids are behind on their chores.

So that's why things are such a mess! I had no idea! Thank you, Chore Monster!

13 RULES OF THE ROOST

Sarah and I had discussed getting backyard chickens at some point, such as when the kids were grown and the tornados had passed.

So I was surprised when a box of chicks showed up at our house the week before Easter. Our oldest son was not yet a teenager.

I was more surprised when two ducklings joined the box of chicks.

Several of our friends had already entered the backyard chicken craze. The more rural their homesteads, the less success they had. It's still a wild west for white meat out there.

I wouldn't know. Unlike most men in the Texas hill country, I have no motion-activated, Internet-accessed, high-resolution game camera on my 3,000-acres deer lease.

Still, I considered hawks, foxes and coons as I designed our coop. Its frame would consist of commercial grade, pressure-treated two by fours. Its walls would extend twelve inches into the earth.

Despite its name, chicken wire simply would not do. I would cover the exterior with half-inch, steel-welded screen wire. My planning stopped just short of a reinforced concrete safe room, the kind preppers put in their basements.

As construction commenced, the chicks and the ducklings roamed half a refrigerator box in our garage.

We soon realized ducks grow faster than chickens and ducks have only one kind of stool: loose.

Duck residue still stains our garage floor.

After the first week, we let the birds get some fresh air in the yard. Of all the predators I had contemplated, "family dog" was not on the list. Neither was "family cat."

But to a Labrador retriever ~~mutt~~ mix, a chick is basically a yellow ball that throws itself. And to a cat, chicks are simply yellow mice.

At first, we fended off friendly fire from Hank and Pumpkin. But we eventually let our guards down. Then, disaster struck.

In three days, Hank eliminated four chicks. The attacks weren't mutilating bloodbaths. Hank's too friendly for that. He basically just played them to death.

We buried the four fallen chickens just days before they were to move into their poultry palace, the coop I had spent three Saturdays perfecting.

About this time, Mr. and Mrs. Mallard began sleeping in the yard. After a couple of weeks of safety, one fell prey to a traditional predator of some type.

As unkind as the predator was, at least he covered the funeral expenses.

The original seven chicks were now down to three, including a rooster, and the two ducklings were now one but not in the biblical sense.

Rather than letting the surviving duck soil the new coop, we released it into the wild at Cibolo Creek. We watched her for several minutes.

Before long, she faced a new predator: mallard eager to start a family. I never knew male ducks basically water board their targets into submission.

Back at the coop, the young rooster started to crow.

It sounded more like a fog horn than the perky "cock-a-doodle-doo" I remembered from the Fisher-Price animal sounds toy I had as a kid.

The young cock prefers the 4:00 AM hour which adds another yet predator to the list: neighbor with gun.

14 NEW DOG BREATHES NEW LIFE…AND DEATH

"She's an 'alpha female,'" the animal shelter director said.

I had never heard the term. I assumed it was similar to "queen bee" or "prima donna." You know, a little annoying, but possibly not a deal breaker.

Our youngest son was six. He had hounded his mother and me for months for a puppy, pun definitely intended.

He was too young to remember when Hank was a puppy, so he wanted his own puppy experience.

He was also too young to remember the thousands of dollars of property damage Hank inflicted upon my estate. I wasn't.

While I had my doubts about the rat terrier / red heeler ~~mutt~~ mix he picked out, I went along with it.

"We got a new puppy," I told a friend a few days later.

"*You* got a new puppy," he corrected. My head dropped under reality's weight.

She's "Lucy." She certainly has the feistiness of Lucille Ball.

She's only a foot high and two and a half feet long, but she can jump and touch a doorknob with her nose. She can't yet turn it, but give her a few months. She's only a puppy.

She actually shouldn't get much bigger – her body, anyway.

Her ears are another story. They're like a Chihuahua's. They pick up Austin TV stations 100 miles away.

What they're not picking up are my instructions to stop biting legs, jumping on houseguests, barking before dawn and urinating on freshly-cleaned carpets. I'm beginning to wonder if "Lucy" is short for "Lucifer."

While I have wanted to return her multiple times, my wife finds redeeming qualities in hard-to-love mammals, including yours truly.

For example, Lucy is a decent walking companion. Heelers really do heel. Hank, however, refuses to cross a bridge, no matter how small.

Of course, Lucy could also drag a leash holder into an oncoming F350. Thank God for those parachute ears to slow her down.

Lucy has certainly breathed new life into Hank, the old eunuch. She nips at his neck and slips under his legs. He climbs on her back and wrestles her in the yard.

She eats his food. He doesn't mind.

On the other paw, Lucy has breathed death into Pumpkin. She traps him under cars and runs him up trees.

He sleeps inside now.

Now about that city ordinance requiring pet licenses. Hank and Pumpkin have their $4 tags of approval. Lucy is yet unsanctioned.

I wonder what Pumpkin had on his mind the other day when I saw him in front of the city pound. That tattle tail! (sic)

I have no idea who would have put him up to it.

I love Lucy.

15 KIDS' SAYING THE DARNDEST THINGS

Each year, I put some of the kids' funny quotes on the back of our family Christmas card. It helps explain the family photo on the front.

"What are you giving up for lent?" I once asked our oldest son, thirteen at the time. "Church," he replied with a mischievous middle school smile.

Our seven-year-old son was catch-and-release fishing once. When we couldn't get a deep hook out of one fish's mouth, we cut the line and threw it back with the hook still in.

"That fish now has a nose ring!"

His twin sister heard her voice bounce off a cliff wall next to the river. She was so excited. "It made a gecko!"

During a recent rain shower, she saw a rainbow while driving down the interstate. "There's a rainbow!" she announced. The road noise kept her twin brother from hearing her clearly.

"Where's Rambo?" he asked.

At a restaurant dinner, I explained that the drinks were not free. "You have to pay for everything you get in life," I said not wanting to pass up a teachable moment.

A seven-year-old needed clarity, "What about if you find it?"

He seems to have an exception for every rule.

His eight-year-old brother once asked a perceptive question: "Does everything at JC Penney's cost a penny?" You would think so given a retail industry turned on its head by e-commerce.

Speaking of money, the twins got some from their grandparents for their birthday. Our son opened the envelope and concluded the $50 check was solely for him. When I explained otherwise, he whined, "But 5 is an odd number. You can't split it!"

When we visited a friend's church, an eight-year-old noticed a similarity between the minister there and our minister at home. "Do you have to be bald to be a preacher?" he inquired.

A few nights ago, I told his little brother to go to bed. His response: "But I haven't yawned yet!"

His sister tried to bend the rules, too.

"Did you brush your teeth?" I asked one night.

"Umm, yes, sir," she replied looking up and off to the right.

"Are you telling the truth?" I quizzed.

She answered while turning toward bathroom, "I think I didn't. Thank you, Dad."

My pleasure.

Later, as I tucked her into bed, she said she didn't want to use the "F-word" to describe an overweight school friend. Instead, she said, "He had a big tummy."

Her older brother doesn't use the F-word either. He prefers the more formal "obeast."

Another time, she explained, "I don't use the word 'butt.' I use 'tooshie' or 'biscuits' or sometimes 'watermelon' or 'cantaloupe.'"

One morning I asked her if she would like some strawberries in her raisin bran. "No, thanks," she said. "I'm not a grown-up yet."

In other fruit news, I once showed her older brother a tangerine and asked, "Would you like one of these?"

"No, thanks, I don't like orangutans," he said. That makes sense. He doesn't like bananas either.

Another brother confided, "I wish my birthday was on September 25th."

"Why?" I asked.

"Because it's Christmas!" he replied, as if I was missing something obvious.

It's not just dates we get turned around. It's words, as well.

Saturday freebies at the grocery store are "examples." The liquid used to clean your hands is "sand hanitizer." Cats do their business in a tray of "kitty glitter." Those bumps on your tongue? They're "taste bugs." And if something upsets your stomach, you'll probably have a "vowel movement."

In the kids' song, "This Little Light of Mine," we sometimes sing, "Hide it under the *bushes*, NO!"

Speaking of plants, the gnat-nabbers are "Venus fly swatters." And those really big flies? They're "horseshoe flies."

But it's not just words we get turned around. It's letters, too.

When Sarah responded to an ill-timed request from a kid with an 'N' - 'O,' one of our sons asked, "What's that spell? 'On'?"

I once received this text from my seven-year-old angel:

"i love you bab"

I love you, too, Angle. (sic!)

And then it's not just words and letters we get wrong. It's numbers, two. (sic!!)

"I know the firefighters' pass code!" a five-year-old said once. "It's 1-1-9!"

Once our nine-year-old son and his friend were playing in a new backyard fort we were building. "This is awesome!" his friend exclaimed. "I give it a ten out of ten."

"Wait," our son replied. "The slide's not on yet. It's just a ten out of nine."

And then there was the time I tried to explain the concept of rational numbers to a sixth grader.

"What's the root word of *rational*?" I asked, expecting to hear "ratio."

The sheer brilliance I received in response:

"Rash?"

16 TEXAS VS YOURS TRULY

"Do you want to play flag football with your coach from last year?" I asked my ten-year-old son.

"No," he replied, much to my surprise. I thought he enjoyed last season.

"I want to play tackle."

His friends are playing tackle. His mom is okay with tackle. A local physician is letting his son play tackle. Our thirteen-year-old is on his third season of tackle.

I'd still prefer flag.

It felt like me versus the whole State of Texas, where Friday Night Lights are as much religion as Sunday morning sermons.

I never played organized football. Dad distracted me with soccer.

But I loved playing backyard football with neighborhood kids – even tackle football. Especially tackle. The physicality of tackling tickles something in a boy's development.

Part of me regrets never knocking heads and testing strength with pads on. It probably would have done me some good.

So which do I want for my sons?

The camaraderie of football is its greatest selling point. The sport is simulated battle and borders on barbarism. It is a modern, somewhat socially acceptable form of gladiation.

For me, however, the attraction of football is not the violence. It's the grace. The streaking and passing; the route running and needle threading. It's not the smashing, bashing and crashing.

Naturally, I like the pad-less seven-on-seven passing leagues teams play in the off-season. I wish there were such non-contact options for the fall.

Some medical professionals and parents restrict little boys from playing tackle, saying their brains and bodies aren't developed enough.

I'm in the opposite camp. I'd rather kids play tackle early when they're like marshmallows bumping into and off of each other, before puberty and testosterone come into play.

Older, stronger muscles create speed, force, impact and contortion that the human body was never meant to absorb. It's basic physics.

And the "better" the equipment gets, the more the equipment becomes a weapon to itself.

Many men live with disabilities, mostly minor, resulting from high school football. One of my friends traveled to and from games in an ambulance. The all-district linebacker/fullback was so banged up he needed treatment before and after every game.

I don't have nagging maladies and I'm thankful. Others do and they're thankful – for their experiences in the arena, for participating in something bigger than themselves. Football in Texas certainly fits that bill.

As for the debate in our home that fall, the State of Texas won. My ten-year-old played tackle.

His little sister provided some comfort to her old man.

After overhearing one of our discussions the dangers of football, she consoled, "Don't worry. I'm not playing high school football."

Evidently, middle school remains an option.

17 WOUNDED WARRIOR SAVES A GAME

The last time the three of us went ninety miles per hour toward a hospital, his mom was the one in pain. This time, our ten-year-old was in pain.

Twenty minutes earlier, his tackle football team, the Warriors, faced its fifth loss in six games.

That is, until this now-wounded Warrior spun down an end zone-bound opponent at the one yard line. In the process, our son landed awkwardly on his left forearm.

"Dr. Stahl, we need you!" came the call from the field. I was actually sitting next to Dr. Stahl in the stands. We were discussing football injury statistics, I'm sure.

The seriousness of a sports injury is inversely proportional to the amount of time before medical personnel is called. In this case, an assistant coach made the diagnosis from the field.

"We've got a broken arm here!"

That's when I quit walking toward the field and started sprinting toward the parking lot, keys in hand.

By the time Dr. Stahl splinted my son's crooked arm, a stadium crewman unlocked a field-side gate. A grimacing free safety lumbered to my amateur ambulance, his mom by his side.

"Don't bother stopping at the emergency room," Dr. Stahl said calmly as we loaded into the van. "Take him straight to

Children's. He's going to need surgery."

We left our three uninjured elementary-aged children in tears along the chain link fence while we hurried off with their injured brother. That's when you know you have great friends.

While one friend kept our kids, another retrieved an insurance card and a change of clothes from our house. By day's end, another would bring a condolence tray of Chik-fil-A nuggets.

Every bump on that thirty-minute ride jolted the dislocated bones of our wounded Warrior.

"When are we going to get there?!?" he cried out between groans.

"Is that it?" he exclaimed as we passed by the The Center for Athletes on Spurs Lane. One would think, especially one still in full pads.

We finally made it to Children's. Once stabilized and full of pain meds, the Warrior had other questions during the five-hour wait for surgery.

"Can I have a Krispy Kreme doughnut?" No, son, I'm sorry.

"How about a sip of water?" No, I'm so sorry.

All common nutrition and hydration wisdom goes out the window when an anesthesiologist is around.

The wait gave us plenty of time to be thankful. For as bad as this day was, it was our first emergency room visit in a combined 43 years of childrearing, 37 of which were boy-rearing.

The wait also gave us time to quiz the pediatric ER nurses. It turns out their slowest times are during San Antonio Spurs basketball games and Dallas Cowboys football games. Their busiest times are the two hours following Spurs and Cowboys games.

Evidently, a lot of parents put off their kids' emergency medical treatment until after the big game.

Sounds like we could have stayed to watch the final minute of the Warriors' game.

Coach informed us later that a goal line stand and a "pick six" interception return for a touchdown gave the Warriors their second win of the season.

It also gave some redemption to their first casualty.

The following day, the wounded Warrior's teammates brought him a signed game ball, some cookies and a multi-tooled pocket knife. "Tough Guy" was engraved on the side.

It was clearly the thought that counted. Have you ever tried opening a pocket knife with just one hand?

18 A WEEKEND IN THE SEA BREEZE

We once spent Easter weekend in Rockport on the Texas coast. Seven of us packed into my Toyota Land Cruiser.

Despite its 200,000th mile coming around the corner, we took it over the minivan. Its rugged nature would play better in the elements.

Beach inflatables filled both the top luggage rack and the luggage shelf that plugs into the trailer hitch.

Ever seen an inflatable kayak? The seasonal inventory buyer at Costco has. He put about 30 "Sea Eagles" in his San Antonio stores five Christmases ago. One of them now sat on top of my SUV.

We rented a house in the middle of Old Rockport. It was a VRBVPO (Vacation Rental By Very Proud Owner).

The cottage was a mile from the man-made Rockport beach, but by the decor inside, you'd think it was on its own island in the Caribbean. Our weekend getaway was brought to us by the color turquoise.

Don't get me wrong, "Sea Breeze Cottage" was worth the money. It just wasn't always worth the wait.

We knew our kids were bigger since we last crammed them in for a trip to the coast, but they were also more mature.

We thought those two factors would cancel each other out.

Silence is golden on road trips with five kids, but it's also frequently broken by "I'm hungry" or "Stop it!" or "How much farther?"

We played a game called "Catch Phrase" to pass the time. The objective is to get your teammates to guess a common phrase without using words from the phrase itself.

An eight-year-old didn't get the message:

"This is a house that's at the beach. It's a blank house."

"This is a day we celebrate mothers."

"This is a pie that's made in a pot. It has chicken in it."

We got some great laughs, and his team got a nice win.

Once we arrived, coastal fishing was high on the agenda. Unfortunately, I'm not much help. Having grown up in a landlocked state, I'm basically a fish out of saltwater.

Thankfully, the Good Lord sent an angel in the form of a retired Texas A&M marine biology professor. For three decades, he doubled as a bay fishing guide. Serendipitously, we met him on a public pier one evening.

He pointed us to a green-lit dock and showed us how to use live shrimp as bait. We nabbed speckled trout until well after dark.

On the way home the next morning, we took a ferry to North Padre Island.

"Why do they call it an island when it's part of Texas?" asked an eight-year-old from the third row.

"Padre Island is a long strip of land that is technically surrounded by the Gulf of Mexico," I explained.

"Why is it called 'Gulf of Mexico?'" the eight-year-old asked. "It should be called 'Gulf of Texas!'"

Somebody call our state rep. It's time for a referendum!

Speaking of referenda, our six-year-old daughter decided one was in order. She polled her brothers from the back seat of the Cruiser, "Who wants a new dad? Raise your hand."

I couldn't bear to watch the election returns through the rearview mirror.

After a minute of suspenseful quiet, her sweet voice cast what may have been the deciding vote: "I don't!"

And with that, a father found the strength to drive another mile.

19 MIDDLE AGE MYTHOLOGY

Our family has never prioritized Halloween. Oh sure, we'll make a party or two. We'll hit a few houses ("hit" in the non-vandal sense).

But our kids' costumes have historically consisted of whatever they can find in the dress up box (race car driver, dinosaur, Elmo).

They can also rummage through the garage where one son found a cardboard box and some paint. He came out a square-headed Olaf from Frozen.

It's the creativity that counts, right?

The real excitement around Halloween has often been The Candy Bowl held the day after Halloween. To the victor of the neighborhood sugar-spiked football game goes the spoils: all the leftover candy in one giant bowl.

One year I splurged on Halloween. October 31 fell on a Saturday. Daylight savings time gave us an extra hour of light and sleep. We decided to go big.

First, we planned to pass out store-bought candy instead of the fruit snacks we collected from the back of the pantry.

Then, we planned a party, inviting a few families to our place for soup and cornbread before Trick-or-Treating.

Finally, and most uncharacteristically, I agreed to spend

hard-earned U.S. dollars on new, not used, costumes. (Thrift store costume purchases have occurred from time to time over the years.)

Don't let your imagination run wild. This didn't mean we surfed Amazon for three weeks selecting every last accessory. It meant we visited Wal-Mart at 10:00 a.m. Halloween morning. I found the available selection pleasantly surprising.

Our five-year-old son requested Superman. Two days earlier, he was the only child at his preschool party not dressed like a superhero, unless, of course, a kangaroo counts as a superhero.

Hello? Has no one heard of Captain Kangaroo? Kangaroos can jump twenty-five feet in a single bound, can't they?

Speaking of captains, his seven-year-old brother requested Captain America. Remarkably, I found both Superman and Captain America costumes in just the right sizes.

I thought my luck was running out when I couldn't locate a "Batgirl" or "Secret Service" outfit, two other requests from the home front.

But then, a costume package caught my eye. It read,

Character: Hercules
Size: Adult

It basically had my name on it.

Initially, I struggled to wrap my mind around paying $22.47 for a costume for myself. Cheap costumes are my forte.

The Halloween before, I had broken my string of twelve straight years as a basketball referee (I called a few games in college) when I bought a pair of white coveralls and went as an infectious disease nurse.

But when I remembered that I had to teach the biblical story of David and Goliath at church the next day, I pulled the trigger. I slayed two giants with one stone.

Back home, Batgirl became a beautiful butterfly with some face paint and sheer wings from the dress up box.

The Secret Service agent stuck a pillow under a white button-down, grabbed a walkie talkie and became Paul Blart, Mall Cop.

As for Hercules, he made his grand entrance at the top of the stairways to mixed reviews.

My five-year-old said my skirt looked like a girl's, my seven-year-old said I needed some fake muscles, my nine-year-old asked, "What in the world is that?" and my twelve-year-old observed, "You're obviously not Goliath."

That's it! Enough with the disrespect! I'm stealing the Almond Joys from all your plastic pumpkins! And you better watch out...Hercules is dressing out for the Candy Bowl!

Well before sunset we patronized a few neighborhood homes. Then, we drove to a tract home subdivision a few miles away. It was a land flowing with Milk Duds and Bits-O-Honey.

And one middle-aged mythological god sent to protect mere morsel-seeking mortals.

20 A GUIDE TO TREAT-GIVING

It seems holiday gift guides hit mailboxes earlier every year.

Sausages, cheeses, pies, steaks. Technology gadgets, leather goods, popcorn. There's no shortage of treat ideas for people you know.

But what about treat ideas for people you don't know?

Before we get carried away with Thanksgiving pie orders and Christmas shopping, let's get Halloween right.

While greeting card companies have driven the prominence of conjured holidays, candy companies have driven the Halloween custom of throwing handfuls of high fructose corn syrup at any kid who comes near your property.

On Halloween night – no, afternoon, heck, maybe even morning – kids start filling pillowcases with bounty. Some teenagers will look like bona fide carpetbaggers.

The candy thing has gone off the insulin charts. We need to get back to a saner Trick-or-Treating time because there's nothing more normal than knocking on strange doors to ask for something sweet to eat.

In response to our national sugar addiction, I recommend the following items in lieu of the customary diabetes-inducing fare:

1. Raisins – You can purchase individual one-inch raisin

boxes, you can buy in bulk and create your own plastic bag-fuls, or you can give a single raisin to each child who darkens your doorway.

Any of the above will freak out your visitors which is the point, correct? And you will subtly help with their post-Halloween digestion.

2. Pennies – Most kids have never seen a penny unless they participate in the "share a penny" program at your local quick mart.

Throw a few pennies in Trick-or-Treaters' pails to create a mysterious jingle effect. The bell tolls, does it not?

Feel free to add a story about where the pennies came from: decomposed eyelids at the city cemetery.

3. Work – Here's your chance to reform the lackluster work ethic of a lost generation. Order ten yards of mulch delivered to your lawn the week before Halloween.

When kids knock, hand them a shovel and tell them to start spreading. When they ask for payment, reinforce that work itself is a gift. They should be thankful.

4. Apples – It's ridiculous that people stopped handing out fruit because of a few bad apples in the 1980s. The chances of actually finding a razor blade in your Halloween apple were, well, razor-thin.

A Fuji apple is sweet enough to satisfy any sweet tooth. Plus, apples are like a virtual teeth brushing.

5. Toothbrushes – Speaking of dental hygiene, toothbrushes are the Trick-or-Treating equivalent of tough love. Kids may see it as party-pooping, but years from now they'll remember you as the neighbor with perspective.

Throw in a travel size tube of toothpaste and your wisdom will become legendary. You may even get some eggs out of it.

***

I admit this list may be too much too soon. If it is and you don't make it to the candy aisle, consider your junk drawer as a source of giveaways: pencils, stickers, trinkets, coupons.

Just stay away from the razor blades.

21 GLUTTON FOR PUNISHMENT

For several years, I chaired our city's chamber of commerce golf tournament.

Before one of the rounds, my second son asked, "Will there be crowds watching?" He and I had just finished watching The Masters.

I paused for a moment, gathered my thoughts, and replied, "Why, yes, son, there will be crowds watching, large crowds, in fact," thinking of all the squirrels, birds, wild turkeys, hole-in-one witnesses and beverage cart workers that could justify my answer.

My favorite vacations usually land me on a golf course. I'm not a scratch golfer by any stretch. I usually answer the question, "Do you play golf?" with "I own a set of clubs."

I love the game about ten per cent of the time. But it's that ten per cent that keeps me coming back.

I can hit 100 errant shots in a round, but, like an addict, I fixate on that one strike that settles straight down a fairway or perfectly on a green.

The game of golf has generated plenty of player / caddie banter over the centuries. Here are my favorite lines.

Golfer: "Do you think I can get there with a 5 iron?"

Caddie: "Eventually."

Club selection is the bane of a golfer's existence. I can approach the ball with quiet confidence, execute a flawless swing and strike the ball in the sweetest of spots. And then watch it land 25 yards in front of or behind the target.

My kids have four or five clubs in their bags. Why do I have fourteen, all so hard to use and so easy to lose?

Golfer: "That can't be my ball; it's too old."
Caddie: "It's been a long time since we teed off, sir."

A leading barrier to golf is the time it requires. I'm not real sure how 18 holes became the standard. Thirteen or fourteen holes would allow me my one good shot without exhausting my energy and my wife's patience.

Four-plus hours away from work and family is certainly a sacrifice. It's also a relatively undivided time to build quality relationships, assuming you're playing with the right people.

Golfer: "Please stop checking your watch all the time. It's distracting."
Caddie: "It's not a watch, sir. It's a compass."

Ponce de Leon's fountain of youth pursuit can't touch my epic searches for lost balls. In a golfer's twisted psyche, a bad shot becomes decent if he can simply locate his ball. A horrible shot becomes respectable if he finds someone else's ball.

Golfer: "I think I'm going to drown myself in the lake."
Caddie: "Can you keep your head down that long?"

The fundamentals of a golf swing seem so simplistic: Don't over-grip, don't over-swing, don't sway, keep your head still, and don't try to kill it. I have executed all this and more in some gorgeous practice swings.

But then, mysteriously, demons overtake in the 6 inches, 6

seconds and 6 thoughts between a practice swing and a live one.

When I top, hook or slice a ball into the next zip code, I start the blame game. Everyone is responsible but me: the cart girl, the president, my parents, the people I'm playing with, and especially my caddie.

Golfer: "You have to be the worst caddie in the world."

Caddie: "I don't think so, sir. That would be too much of a coincidence."

22 A TREASURE TROVE

As a writer, I have journals and notebooks and note cards scattered all over the place. I discovered one journal in the side pocket of an old briefcase I hadn't used in years.

I felt like I had happened upon a Dead Sea scroll. Why, yes, I do consider my kids' one-liners holy.

The unearthed notebook's first entry date was Christmas 2014. After opening all the presents, our oldest son, twelve at the time, said, "Wait. Is that it?"

Our second son offered a similar line of questioning, "Did I get anything else?"

Our youngest son evidently hadn't reached the age of jade: "I hope there are presents under the tree tomorrow."

"There won't be," our third son replied. Hope deferred makes a heart sick, the Good Book says, particularly on Christmas morning.

Our sons' little sister was more curious about how Santa worked:

"Does Santa have any friends?"

"Did you keep any of Santa's texts?"

"Mom, do you believe in Santa?" she once asked.

"I believe in the story of Santa," her mother deftly replied.

"It's a yes or no question, Mom," she answered, a bit

perturbed.

Our little girl believes in Santa, but she's not above a lie.

"Did you eat one of those cupcakes?" I asked her once.

"No," she replied.

"Then how did icing get all over your face?" I inquired.

She thought for a minute and said, "My brother threw a cupcake at me."

If she weren't so cute, she'd be easier to discipline.

The questions in a houseful of kids flow like water.

"Do doctors get sick?"

"Dad, was there ice cream when you were a kid? Were there shakes?"

"How long is fifteen minutes?

"How big is a Berenstain bear?"

"When we die, do we turn into a dog or a cat?"

I have tried to make clear that God sent Jesus so that we might live with him forever.

"MIGHT live?" a perceptive son asked. He was looking for a more certain salvation.

The journal reads on with more kid questions. For example, this one from a six-year-old son: "Dad, why do you take a bath every day?"

"Because dads sweat more than kids," I answered.

"Do dads sweat more than grandpas?" he wondered.

I'll let him know in a few years.

Around a campfire eating s'mores one night, one son made up a joke, "What did the kid say after he ate s'mores? I want s'more!"

Around the dinner table, we often play "high-low" where you give your day's best and worst.

Our most succinct son once summarized his day this way, "My good news is I have no bad news. My bad news is I have no good news."

He's on his way to grasping Solomon's wisdom in Ecclesiastes 7:18, "Whoever fears God will avoid all extremes."

23 LESSONS FROM A FAMILY CAMPOUT

Every fall we go camping with four other families. We pack SUVs and minivans and caravan through Utopia, Texas, - yes, Utopia - to Leakey, Texas, and Garner State Park.

Here's the math:

1. Five families times 3.6 kids per family equals 1 heckuva good time.

2. The sum of sweltering heat, record drought and possible wildfires is less than the fun of a weekend on the Frio River.

3. A few days in nature has a disproportionately greater didactic impact than an equal amount of time in civilization.

4. Just outside the circle of comfort lies a geometric spread of shapes not found in urban squares.

Because of the drought, the Frio River wasn't full but it wasn't empty. Fish, all be they smaller, still swam. Skunks still scavenged. Park rangers still fibbed (bears and mountain lions had been seen in the area). Lessons were still learned, including these:

1. We're all in this together.

Twenty-eight people shared one commercial refrigerator for four days. To be overprotective of your OREOs is to be disappointed by the power of human hunger.

Happiness comes from a generous heart and a firm faith in

God's ability to provide.

2. A little dirt won't kill you, though it may endanger your perfectionism.

Watching my offspring crawl into sleeping bags with filthy feet once rattled my sanitized world. I was convinced they would wake with shingles or bed bugs or scabies. When they didn't, I found the courage to let them play in stagnant water.

3. Talent includes a bike-riding three-year-old.

Our Saturday night talent show featured jokes, skits, songs and tricks.

But no act was more pleasurable than a little girl with a big smile riding her training-wheeled bicycle across a mess hall "stage." Giftedness is all around us, if we have the perspective to enjoy it.

4. If you didn't remember to bring it, you don't need it.

Contemporary culture blurs the line between needs and wants.

Camping offers an easy distinction: Your necessities are those items you remembered while packing. Your wants are those you remembered on the way to camp.

Clean underwear made it in. A box fan did not. We survived.

5. Nature has a rhythm. It's best to live by it.

The river flowed lowly and slowly, but constantly. The oaks dropped acorns on the tin roof each morning.

Besides humankind, no other piece of creation strives to do more than it was made to do. If a tireless God rested, if his son routinely escaped to the hills, we should, too.

6. Old habits die hard.

On the drive home, we were not in the car two minutes before one child requested music from the radio. Another asked to play Angry Birds. Once we got home, a five-year-old asked immediately to go to "Toys 4 Us."

Without ready access to rocks and rivers and trees and hills, plastic becomes the coin of the realm.

We slide plastic credit cards and fill our garages - then storage units - with plastic stuff. Clutter quickly buries both the camping equipment and our inner peace.

But a long weekend at a cold river reminds us that nothing levels a mood swing quite like a rope swing.

24 ONTO THE FIELD OF DREAMS

For many years I have coached Little League baseball. I'm quite the combination of intensity and cluelessness. I have the heart of a champion and the skill of a benchwarmer.

When my middle school baseball coach told me I'd never get to play but I could still be on the team, I took him up on it.

"Playing is overrated," I reasoned. "Practice is where character is forged!"

As a coach, I draft for character. But I don't think my teams would look much different if I drafted for skill.

Baseball talent is about as easy to evaluate as figure skating talent. You know if they fall down, but otherwise, you can't really tell them apart. This makes the Little League team selection process all the more comical. Here's a summary:

On a cold Saturday in late February, twenty grown men spend four hours judging how well nine-year-olds field ground balls.

Two nights later, the men gather in a musty motel meeting room to make their selections. Spreadsheets and algorithms hum in the background.

The intensity is completely justified. Two months' worth of self-esteem is riding on this draft.

Online fantasy baseball limits possible ridicule to a small

circle of friends.

Youth baseball coaching puts one's knowledge and skills on display for an entire community to see.

I understand why parents and grandparents love Little League games. There is something mesmerizing, even intoxicating, about watching one's offspring execute a force out.

Kids keep coaches on their toes as much as the other way around. You never know what you're going to get.

A coach once instructed a player to take right field.

"Coach?" the kid asked. "Is that your right or my right?"

I once told a player to get the catcher's gear on. Five minutes later, he was fully armored and standing next to me in the dugout. All the other players had taken the field.

"Where do you want me, Coach?"

"Catcher, son. Catcher."

I like a man who makes no assumptions.

Simplicity and authenticity are what make youth sports so enjoyable. They're why the Little League World Series makes such good TV.

No contracts, no endorsements, no pouting prima donnas. Just innocent kids trying to find their way home.

In Little League, the game ball is more memorable than the final score. The concession stand candy lineup is more important than its batting counterpart.

I'll try to remember all this next season when we finish 7 and 7 and place 5th in the tournament.

I've coached long enough to win a trophy or two. But they don't outshine the faces of kids who allowed me the thrill of leading them onto the field of dreams.

25 PUTTING THE 'COACH' IN COACH PITCH

After several years of coaching my oldest son in "kid pitch," I got sent to the minors. I agreed to lead a "coach pitch" team again.

It had been several years since I coached at that level. I wondered if the coaches would be less wound up than they were several years before.

They weren't. Some of them might as well have been wearing stirrups.

These guys really put the "coach" in "coach pitch."

"I'm just trying to teach my kids error-free baseball," one of them told me.

Wrong league, sir. Barring a birth certificate scam, you have all six- and seven-year-olds like the rest of us.

"We haven't had one clean inning. I want a clean inning!" another coach yelled to his team.

His team subsequently made five errors and gave up three runs along with the lead.

Somewhere along the way, many coaches – and parents, for that matter – have forgotten that we learn the most when we succeed the least.

Some coaches are more covert, but their driven-ness clearly communicates that winning is everything. It's as if their egos and their legacies are on the line.

They stretch base running rules to the point baseball looks more like track. They banish ballplayers to the bench or the outfield, never letting them see the light of infield day.

They forget – or never learned – that the real objectives are fun and character formation. Baseball is still a game, though for some kids it feels like a job.

Some kids are bucking the trend. They're hanging up the cleats and picking up the golf clubs…at age eleven. Like a corporate manager nearing retirement, these kids have had enough of the stress. They're hitting the links to relax.

Of course, not all coaches are over the top. Many keep things in perspective.

A retired Little League coach suggested this strategy: "I told my parents at the start of every season, 'Out of all the kids on our team, only one will play high school baseball.'"

Surely he meant only one will play professionally.

"No, I meant high school," he reiterated.

That's what's so spellbinding about the state of modern youth sports. It's like we've shelved old-fashioned statistics alongside the old wooden bats.

Or maybe we know the odds. We just think our progeny can beat them. Hubris is a formidable opponent.

Ironically, honest college coaches will tell you the cream rises to the top regardless of a coach's zealotry or a parent's pressure.

With some relief, we can cure the obnoxiousness that taints the nation's pastime at the lowest levels. The Little League pledge, penned in 1954, is a good place to start:

"I trust in God / I love my country and will respect its laws / I will play fair and strive to win / But win or lose I will always do my best."

Now that's a grand slam.

26 PUTTING THE 'YOUTH' IN YOUTH SPORTS

The first-time tee ball mother really didn't know.

"Is it normal for a tee ball team to practice twice a week? I mean, he's only five."

"They won't have any practices once the season begins," I consoled. I didn't have the heart to tell her why: They'll be playing two games a week.

Two generations ago, youth sports consisted of a pickup truck rumbling around town picking up kids to play a similarly aggregated group in the next town over.

No parents watched. No grandparents came. Uniforms were like-colored t-shirts. Hats were a luxury, as were gloves that fit. My left-handed father played catcher with a right-hander's mitt.

There were no all-stars or state tournaments. Most fields didn't have backstops or fences. There were only kids competing for the love of the game.

We've progressed since then. We have dugouts and pitching machines. Parents do the signing up. Grandparents do the cheering on. I am thankful for the advancements and the people who made them happen.

But modern youth sports highlight how kid-centric much of

American life can be. Parents view their children as extensions of, even judgments on, themselves. A relentlessly culture of comparison certainly drives the tendency.

Families travel hours for a nine-year-old football game. Weekends revolve around a ten-year-old's tournament. Parents pay thousands of dollars for personal coaching and competitive leagues.

I'll admit it: I get more of a surge than I should from watching my six-year-old shoot a basketball. I need help, too.

From inside the pressure cooker, I try to remember this paradox: the most impactful moments of life are unplanned and unorganized.

It won't be the hit or the catch that a kid remembers. It will be the snack after the game. He or she will more likely recall a campout under the stars than a game under the lights.

My eight-year-old son saw a Cub Scout flyer at school once. "I want to do that next year," he told his mother.

"You won't be able to play any sports then," she replied.

"That's fine."

That's fine?!? But what about your place on the depth chart? Your chances of making the high school team? Your plans to play in the NFL? I hope he's thought through the implications.

A successful businessman told me about his teenage daughter's nascent golf career. She plays in tournaments all over the country.

"Golf is the easiest sport for girls to get a scholarship in," said the man who likely needed little assistance paying for his daughter's education.

His comment brought into focus one final irony: Considering the grueling business of modern collegiate athletics, would I want that life for my child anyway?

A healthy perspective probably replies, "Probably not."

27 WHAT'S FOR DINNER?

The old man's kids were long grown and gone. But he recalled some research he had seen as a young father.

"Frequency of family dinners is the number one predictor of SAT scores," he told me. "I used to make each of my kids talk for five minutes at the dinner table every night."

The regular family gathering is nearly extinct in our overextended American culture. Disconnection runs rampant in our time.

"Together alone" typifies our technologically-networked, but emotionally-fragmented, lives. Nevertheless, connection remains critical to parent and child wellbeing.

Many young people seek connection and meaning from their social networks. They simply seek transportation and financing from biological ones.

But a Creative Designer put us in biological groups to meet both physical and emotional needs.

Bellingham, WA, minister Matthew McCoy has studied the role of eating habits in spiritual and personal formation:

"Daily rhythms, when looked at on any individual day, seem almost insignificant. But when taken over the course of a lifetime, they are a massive part of how our identities, and thus our ethics, are formed," McCoy said.

"What we eat demonstrates who we think we are and how we relate to each other, to all living things, to science and to God," he continued. "I can say whatever I like about what I believe, but when it is dinner time, all can see if I am telling the truth."

Over the years, I've fed my kids their fair share of chicken fingers on a sports bleacher. We've consumed plenty of hot dogs and hamburgers on the way to practices and plays.

The rushed eating has sometimes left our kids confused.

"It's green. It must be a vegetable," our daughter once said once ... about a pear.

On plenty of days we only eat from the 'O' food group: Cheerios, Eggo's, Spaghetti Os, Cheetos, Oreos, et cetero (sic!).

One time I left a leftover food pizza in the trunk of my car for two weeks. When I finally discovered it, the pie had shown zero signs of decomposing. It did not smell. It looked the same.

"How long does this preservative-ridden food stay in my body?" I wondered.

When our family does sit down for dinner, it doesn't always go well. Kids irritate each other with smacking and other bad habits.

"He needs cotillion!" our daughter once said to her older brother. I forget what he was doing. Probably using his fingers as a serving spoon.

Sibling rivalries can take center stage.

"Was it fun playing your sister in chess?" I asked a brother.

His annoying reply: "It was easy."

But all of our hearts really hunger for relationship and community.

If we can get past the initial revulsion to work, both parents and kids end up wanting to contribute to the planning, preparing and putting away of the family meal. Plus, food always tastes better when we work for it.

I've noticed this cumulative effect to family meals: The more you have, the better they get.

All family members – even the littlest – learn their chores. Conversation habits improve. Interruptions decrease. Respect increases.

Controlling the pace of life is a great challenge for modern families. Committing to family meals at home is swimming upstream.

"Many other demands must be met in a day," Mr. McCoy says. "The schedule is so full, the food budget is so small, and exhaustion is an ever present companion."

But where there's a will, there's a way, as they say.

One father I know made breakfast the family meal, rising early to make it hot every day. Another mother gathers her ducklings for dessert after an active evening.

"I make us all sit down and look at each other for ten or fifteen minutes," she told me. "It's a small thing but it makes a big difference."

Physicians will tell you: Many of our physical ailments have emotional roots, and many of our mental ailments affect us physically. We desperately need answers to our questions.

Like an old Bible, the dining table has answers if we'd just dust it off, answers for the SAT and for life.

28 HELP FOR THE OVER-COMMITTED

Do you have more tasks than time? More obligations than energy? More demands than endurance? Are your commitments spread too wide and yourself too thin?

If you respond to "How are you?" with "busy," if you often think, "Just let me get through this, then things will slow down," this chapter is for you.

Maintaining a reasonable and sustainable pace of life is a ubiquitous challenge.

No one could imagine fifty years ago the options available to us today. With fast food and cell phones and networked files, not to mention caffeine in dozens of forms, we can work until the cows come home – and until they get milked and go to sleep and wake up.

Besides work, we can also fill untold hours with for-profit networking and non-profit volunteering.

Parents face the brunt of the modern schedule assault. Traditional activities (e.g., Little League) have elevated to "select" teams and "travel ball." Formerly obscure activities (e.g., lacrosse) have become commonplace.

Name the sport, musical instrument or interest and I bet private tutoring is available, with a college scholarship hanging in the balance.

It's all well and good until it all becomes too much.

We parent through our car's rear view mirror. The dinner table becomes surface storage. An evening with nothing to do feels like a waste of time.

I can't remember when I last uttered the phrase, "I'm bored." I detested boredom as a child. I fantasize about it as an adult.

Boredom is obviously not the goal. Balance is. Here are two truths from physiology that I learned from my circuit training class at the YMCA. They help us maintain balance in our schedule.

#1: The stronger you are, the better your balance will be.

Before I started the YMCA class, I could not put on a sock while standing on one foot without tipping over like a sippy cup. I would hop around searching for something vertical to back into.

But the stronger my leg muscles become, the more stably I can stand on one foot and slip a sock on the other. Likewise, a balanced schedule requires saying "no" to time-consuming activities, even well-meaning ones.

Saying "no" requires strength. It may offend someone or preclude you from future opportunities. Even so, the results are worth the risks. You will stay rested, relaxed and ready for your highest priorities.

#2: The more focused you are, the better your balance will be.

Some exercises in my circuit training class require standing on one foot.

The trainer instructs us to focus on a spot on the floor or on an inanimate object on the wall. If we look at our swaying neighbor, we're more likely to lose our balance. Focusing on something immovable steadies us.

Likewise, if you stay focused on your established goals, on your anchor of faith, on things that do not sway or change, you will stay upright. You will stand firm. You will remain balanced.

Balance holds at bay the stress that comes from over-commitment.

When inevitable stressors do appear, balance provides the

emotional and physical margin to handle them, keeping collateral damage like broken and damaged relationships at bay.

29 HELP FOR THE UNDER-COMMITTED

A family counselor once told me if marriage were a house, commitment would be its foundation. The longer I'm married, the more I believe there is no greener grass than commitment.

Commitment is where children play freely and where love strolls wholeheartedly. It's the soft carpet on which the hard knocks of life can fall.

Most failed marriages once proclaimed the traditional wedding vow "...for better or worse, for richer or poorer, in sickness and in health, 'til death do us part."

But then things changed. Circumstances changed. People changed.

In some respects, marriage seems like a cruel joke. You marry and your mate begins to decline. He gains weight. She gains wrinkles. He goes bald. She goes gray. He loses his strength. She loses her mind.

As we all have heard, a new marriage in America – even in church – has the chance of a coin flip.

Perhaps the following update to the traditional wedding vow would paint a clearer picture of the covenant necessary to beat the odds.

As the late Abilene Christian University professor Dr. Charles Siburt said at the wedding of one of his sons, "Your love does not uphold the covenant. The covenant upholds your love."

***

I, Bride, take you, Groom, to be my lawful wedded husband, to have and to hold from this day forward...

...in good years and bad, through pay raises and unemployment, whether fit or fat, whether straight up or bent over, whether bald or hairy and when both bald and hairy, in good smells and bad, whether helpful in the kitchen or comatose on the couch, in hunting season and out, during conflict with family and camaraderie with friends, through long hours at work and lonely hours at home.

I will choose to love you when I don't feel like looking at you and you don't listen to me, when kids overrun our lives and days overrun our nights, when things don't go as planned and I wouldn't choose you again if given the chance.

I will stay committed. I will stay the course. I will believe in you more than you believe in yourself.

For as long as we both shall live. 'Til death do us part.

***

And I, Groom, take you, Bride, to be my lawful wedded wife, to have and to hold from this day forward...

...in good years and bad, through emotions and tears and illogical fears, when babies come and leave their mark, whether dinner gets made or laundry gets done, when my family drives you crazy and my driving makes you mad, whether supportive or negative, whether joyful or needy.

When I don't feel like listening to you and you can't stand to look at me, when the jokes that once made you giggle make you mad as a hornet, when I can do no right and your family can do no wrong, when I get home late and your day starts early, when kids misbehave and I'm not much better.

I will stay committed. I will stay the course with faith that two can become one and not ever be two again.

For as long as we both shall live. 'Til death do us part because to part would be, well, death.

30 BE REDUNDANT

I thought my buddies and I were the ones roughing it.

Four dads in Big Bend National Park. Three days of backpacking. Three nights in tents. No showers. No home-cooked meals. Just freeze dried food and compostable toilets. Oh, and wild bears within fifty feet of camp.

Only later did it occur to me: The four of us left four women to care for a combined fourteen pre-school and elementary-aged children for four straight days.

Now, who was roughing it?

The term "redundancy" has seen a resurgence in recent years. It means backup.

If one Internet line goes down, another becomes available. If one hard drive goes bad, another has the files backed up. Service without interruption.

But redundancy isn't a human idea. In the natural world, we see many examples.

We have not one eye, but two. Not one arm, but two. Not one lung, but two. Not one kidney…

If one part goes down, our bodies can often still function on another.

Plants get their nutrients from the sun and the soil. Like the omnivorous bears my friends and I confronted in Big Bend, most of us get our nutrients from both plants and meat.

We see redundancy in government.

If you live in the city and the police won't respond to your concern, you can call the county sheriff. If you live in the county and the sheriff doesn't respond, you can call the constable.

On a national level, if Congress makes a law that infringes on our rights, the Supreme Court can throw it out. If the President thinks a law is a bad idea, he vetoes it. The framers wanted checks and balances. They required redundancy.

Transatlantic telegraphs didn't become useful when the first line was laid in 1858. They became viable when multiple cables were submerged in the 1860s. With redundancy came reliability.

Without redundancy, life goes haywire. Information stops. Bodies become disabled. Dictators take over. Needs go unmet.

Which brings me to my realization about who really roughed it that weekend in the woods.

It was our wives.

My heart goes out to single mothers and fathers. They need our honor, encouragement and support.

While some people single-parent by choice, others do it through no fault of their own. Many do it well. Few would say it's easy.

Remarkably, some people still largely view single-parenting as an equal means to raising children.

Two parents create redundancy, and redundancy keeps balls from being dropped, kids from being neglected, teachable moments from being missed.

Of the four guys on the Big Bend trip, two had come from divorced homes and two had come from intact marriages. The national divorce rate played out in our midst.

But, to a man, each is trying to create a home built on a vibrant marriage, a home that offers kids two sources of love and care.

In other words, we're trying to be redundant.

31 CONFESSIONS OF AN INTROVERT

For many years I considered myself an extrovert. I tried to be friends with everyone. I won citizenship awards. I people pleased.

Home, church and school reinforced the behavior. The more friendly, the more mature; the more mature, the more Christian.

The more outgoing, the more destined for influence and success. Shyness was a pathology to overcome, not a signal to some inner strength.

Culture laid the groundwork. If nineteenth century America was a culture of character, twentieth century America, with the rise of entertainment stars and salesmanship programs, became a culture of personality.

According to Susan Cain, author of "Quiet: The power of introverts in a world that can't stop talking," a third to a half of the U.S. population is introverted.

By introverted, Cain doesn't mean hermit, black trench coats or multiple personalities. She doesn't mean anti-social.

She means people who get more energy from being alone or in a small group than from being in a crowd. She means people who think first and talk second.

Introverts tend to dive into a problem like a pelican toward a fish. They prefer to write out a response rather than impromptu speak. They favor uninterrupted concentration to multi-tasking, and working alone to working in groups.

Modern life has left little room for the introvert's natural habitat. Starting in kindergarten, desks are grouped into pods. High school and college students are placed into study groups.

Professional workplaces have open-aired cubes and open door policies. The central idea? The more stimulation, the better.

Not so, says Cain who claims creativity is actually stifled in group settings where the biggest egos or the most eloquent communicators lead masses into "groupthink."

It's no footnote, she says, that history's two leading technology empires were largely born of the solitary study by their introverted co-founders: Bill Gates of Microsoft and Steve Wozniak of Apple.

Still, business schools champion leaders who "light up the room" with larger-than-life personas. Students are expected to think out loud all day and mingle in social settings into the night. A quiet evening of reflection is viewed as falling behind.

Ironically, it was in my own MBA program that I first discovered my introversion. Previously, I diagnosed my desire to work alone, my fatigue from "working a room," my bent toward the contemplative life, as burnout or even depression.

I would self-talk myself back into a social mood with contemporary wisdom about the importance of networking. "It's not what you know, but who you know…"

But in that graduate school class I allowed myself to answer a personality test honestly. I didn't try to game it into the personality type a promising young executive should exhibit.

The result? I was one of two introverts in the 25-student cohort. My terror was only mitigated by the fact that the other introvert was a suave salesman of business intelligence software and arguably the coolest guy in the class.

Today, I try to trust my deeper desires. I enjoy working with people, but my renewal comes from being alone. I try to remember that saying "no" to a world that can't stop talking can mean saying "yes" to so much more.

32 MORE DARNDEST THINGS

Following church one Sunday, we milled around with other young parents outside the lobby doors. After a while we couldn't seem to locate our third son who was four years old.

Eventually, we found him – with a big smile on his face – urinating like a cherub in a flowerbed.

We needed frequent opportunities to teach this youngster bathroom etiquette. For a time he was using toilet paper without tearing it off. A single flush would carry down half a roll of toilet paper.

I suspect it was this son who suctioned a plunger on the hood of my car before work one day.

A family friend once caught him eating his "nasal produce," for lack of a better term.

"Does that taste good?" she asked him.

"Best food on earth," the little guy replied.

Once he explained to me that if you have dirt under your fingernails, "you can pick your nose and it will clean them."

Another time he asked his mom, "Can you survive on boogers?"

He will likely need to watch his sodium intake later in life.

He once offered the following nutritional philosophy: "Healthy foods make your muscles strong. Sweet foods make your muscles big."

His younger brother is often interested in the origin of foods.

"Dad, where do hot dogs come from? Are they the cow's weenie?"

His twin sister is also interested: "Does white milk come from white cows and chocolate milk from brown cows?"

As a five-year-old, a brother once told me in no uncertain terms, "Dad, I need to watch Toy Story 2."

"Do you NEED to watch Toy Story 2 or do you WANT to?" I asked in a leading question that I hoped would inspire mature perspective.

"I need to," he answered.

Nice try, Dad.

When our oldest son was three, the original Toy Story was his favorite movie. One time his grandparents couldn't find their copy of the movie while babysitting him. Instead, they popped in the wedding video of their oldest daughter, my wife.

"There's my mommy and my daddy!" our son exclaimed. "Am I going to be baby Jesus?!?"

Raised in a heyday of Texas Longhorns football, the sport quickly became a big deal to our two oldest sons.

As a four-year-old, our second son followed NFL teams as best he could. In his vernacular, the Green Bay Packers were the "Graham Crackers."

His older brother would sometimes make him cry on the front yard field. On one such occasion, I heard the following plea from the six-year-old as the four-year-old entered the house crying.

"I'll make you a deal!" the older brother yelled from outside the house. "You can have the ball back on the one yard line, but it's fourth down!"

After receiving no response, the older brother gritted his teeth.

"Come on! It's not about winning and losing! It's about having fun!"

Oh, is that right, Mr. Firstborn?

33 A TRIBUTE TO MOMS

For all the motivational experts and purveyors of inspiration, moms have the original fire in the belly. They are the original incubators.

For all the entrepreneurs and startup junkies, for all the adventure sport fanatics, for all the seventh grade boys looking for their first date to a dance, moms are the world's biggest risk takers.

They give of themselves, literally and figuratively, in the face of endless potential harms.

They bring life into a world that's fraught with death. They nurture life until it can stand on its own, with no guarantee that it will, in fact, stand.

Motherhood, wherever it may be found, is a purely remarkable feat. May it be forever honored, first by fathers, then by children. Without it, the world simply would not go on.

When I think of Mom, I think of soft hands and back scratches.

I love her back scratches so much that I once dreamed of inventing an automatic back scratcher – complete with her nails and her ideal pressure – for when life would take me beyond her reach but not beyond the need for comfort.

When I think of Mom, I think of macaroni and cheese and

Smiley Stew, the ground beef and beans I refused to eat before its creative rebranding. I think of leftovers and a microwave.

"Better a small serving of vegetables with love than a fattened calf with hatred," Proverbs 15:17 says.

I think of Easy Listening 92.9 FM. The music soothed Mom's stress in bumper-to-bumper traffic. It gave me a headache.

I think of Extra sugar-free gum and white Tic Tacs, the ones that tasted sweet for a minute and then quickly turned to menthol overkill.

I think of her dread of Sunday nights and the kindergarten lesson plans the principal required.

I get it. Just how many ways can you say, "This week we are studying the color purple?"

I think of a canoe trip down the Buffalo River and her pleading with my father to keep our canoe right-sized. She could not swim, and she could not get her perm wet.

Ours was the only canoe in the group that did not tip.

I think of swimming lessons and her walking backwards to give me more practice even when I begged her to stand still. She knew what was best for me.

I think of Perry Como vinyls and an Amy Grant concert.

I think of her sitting next to my bed on nights I was scared or sick. I think of the hum of the humidifier and amoxicillin's aftertaste.

I think of the snowy day she called the city fire department to our county property.

She had smelled the neighbor's chimney, saw steam rising from my father's workshop and felt its sunbaked dark red door. She wanted to keep us safe. The false alarm cost us $200.

The late Rich Mullins' music career and free spirit took him far and wide. But they never took him outside the reach of a mother's love.

In "I'll Carry On," he wrote, "I'll carry the songs I learned when we were kids. I'll carry the scars of generations gone by. I'll pray for you always, and I'll promise you this: I'll carry on, I'll carry on."

34 DADS ACCORDING TO KIDS

After a pre-Mother's Day shopping trip with two of my sons, one of them asked a question that doubled his allowance on the spot.

"Dad?" he asked, "when is Father's Day?"

I seized the opportunity to tell them the following joke. They didn't really get it.

Question: Why is Father's Day six weeks after Mother's Day?

Answer: Some guys were shooting the bull about a month after the first Mother's Day when, all of a sudden, one of them stood up and said, "Hey! Wait a minute!"

Men in general are easy targets. Dads are particularly so.

"Dad," read my Father's Day card one year, "When God made you, he made the world a much better place…a little weirder, maybe, but much better."

Thanks.

I once happened upon one of our family photographs hanging on a wall. A t-shirt had been cut out of printer paper and taped across my torso.

The paper t-shirt had a nine-year-old's handwriting on it:

World's
Greatest
~~Father~~
Farter

Cruel and unusual!

If you want the truth about anything, you ask kids. Their filters simply aren't fully developed.

Age is certainly not off limits.

I asked my twelve-year-old son if he would like to go with me to say happy birthday to a neighbor who was turning ninety.

"No, thanks," he said. "He's more in your age range."

According to my eight-year-old daughter, "you know you're old when you start mixing cereals."

Neither is physical appearance off limits.

After looking at the back of my head of thinning hair, a five-year-old son said, "Dad, you have a Bob spot!"

His twin sister was no less observant from the front.

"Daddy?" she said, "Did you know you can cut your eyebrows? They're so big! They're like a monster! Can I braid them?"

Fortunately, their nine-year-old brother had more acute awareness on his Father's Day questionnaire at church. He's proud of his dad… "because he has a six pack."

Attaboy, son! You're getting the power tools!

He was also asked, "What was your dad like as a child?"

"Handsome," he wrote. He must see himself in me.

There was confusion on the church questionnaires about their dad's favorite food. The younger kids said "broccoli" while the older kids said "pizza."

Their father evidently has difficulty aligning his words and actions. Do as I say, kids, not as I do!

According to the Father's Day surveys, my kids love their dad because "he makes cupcakes" and he is "so pleasant."

In my free time, I go "to a hotel," and, if I were a cartoon character, I would be "Bugs Bunny."

When asked, "What is something your Dad always says?" my

eight-year-old daughter said, "No bueno."

When asked the same question, my nine-year-old son responded, "This is unacceptable."

Well, of course it's unacceptable! My kids will never develop into their hereditary six packs if they eat pizza all the time! What's up, Doc!?!

On second thought, I wish he had responded with something like: "I love you, son. I am really happy with you."

A great thing about life is there's always next year. And Hallmark will make sure next year has a Father's Day...about a month after Mother's Day.

35 SCREENING SCREEN TIME

"Can we discourage teachers from asking for iPads for five-year-olds?" a fellow board member asked.

She and I serve together with a local education group that raises money for our local public schools.

Several heads nodded in agreement with the spirit of the question.

It's the same spirit that makes me cringe when I see a two-year-old staring at a cell phone. Such scenes prompt "no wonder" moments, as in, "No wonder our society is struggling."

While the original cathode ray tube screens were introduced decades ago, the last two decades have seen an explosion of screens.

With modern screens' declining cost and inclining definition, it's hard to look anywhere without seeing a screen of some size, shape or pixilation.

For example, consider a modern-day medical office visit:

1. A sign-in clipboard? Nope, here's an electronic tablet to register with.

2. A piece of fine artwork hanging on the wall? Forget about it. We'll display promotions on a jumbo flat screen.

3. A magazine for you, ma'am? No, thank you. I have some texts to respond to and some feeds to peruse.

The ubiquity of screens has introduced messaging that's full of emoticons and extreme abbreviations.

An in-person chat with my fourteen-year-old revealed key truncations that every parent should know.

Dad to son: "What are some abbreviations you use in your text message chats?"

Son: "Do you mean shortcuts?"

Dad: "Yes, I mean shortcuts. Thank you for reducing my syllable count by sixty per cent."

"Sure, Dad," he responded, offering the following *shortcut* definitions:

1. wyd – "What are you doing?" Warning: If the answer to this question is something exciting, it may lead to…

2. fomo – "Fear of missing out"

3. wbu – "What about you?" as in, "I'm going to the county fair this weekend. What about you?"

4. nvmd – "Nevermind" as in "old news"

5. ikr - "I know, right?" A phrase of agreement

6. rly – "Really?"

7. fr tho – "For real, though" as in, "no joke"

8. tmr – "Tomorrow"

9. lol – "Laughing out loud" This truncation hangs on after many years, though most smartphones now convert it to tears streaming down a smiley face emoji.

Emojis and animojis (i.e., animal emojis) are the domain of smartphones.

Flip phones are out of luck and out of style which is precisely why my friend purchased one for his middle school daughter recently.

"I don't think she takes it out much," he surmised with dry wit. "It's more for my convenience than for her entertainment."

There's a novel idea: An adult acting like one. How functional.

If there was ever a time for adults to play adults, it's now. If I told you things some middle schoolers do with their devices, it would make your heart skip a beat – if it didn't break first.

Kids need restrictions. Giving them unabated access to the

Internet is like subleasing a room in your home to an adult bookstore.

Non-technical boundaries help, too, such as no screens in non-public places, particularly bedrooms.

To borrow an ~~abbreviation~~ shortcut from contemporary culture, parents should not try to be GOATs (greatest of all time). Kids respond best, over time, to boundaries and "tough love."

Parents should offer the kind of personal engagement that makes screens, and the conversations on them, a little less mesmerizing.

With strong relationships and up-front communication, kids won't have a need for this shortcut: psos – "Parent standing over shoulder."

They'll have integrity no matter who's looking.

36 MAKING CONTENTMENT LESS ELUSIVE

One summer, our family took a ski boat ride from a friend's lake house.

Our seven-year-old son surveyed the lake houses lining the shore. He noticed some of them had swimming pools.

"Hey, Dad," he said. "Why do those houses need a pool when they have the lake?"

Perceptive question, I thought. My reply had something to do with the desire to swim in a more controlled environment. He seemed to get it. Sort of.

Being content with what we have is a perpetual challenge. Global and social media combine to constantly show us what we're missing.

Wanting what others have is not a modern dilemma. Thousands of years ago, Moses etched a commandment on a stone tablet: "Don't set your heart on anything that is your neighbor's." (Exodus 20:17 MSG)

The temptation to covet is not just reserved for things. Experiences and opportunities are also at play.

Disney World has been the talk in our home recently. We've had a few friends visit the Magic Kingdom.

"Is Disney World in Texas?" one brother asked.

"No, it's in Boston," his seven-year-old sister informed him.

Boston? Okay. The farther, the better, as far as I'm concerned. It keeps life simpler.

The founder of outdoor gear maker Patagonia, Yvon Chouinard, did not set out to build a $200 million a year company when he started in the early 1970s. He simply wanted to create higher quality rock climbing apparel and equipment than what was available at the time.

The multi-millionaire still speaks of a simplicity paradox. He encourages people to have fewer possessions of better quality that last longer.

It's not a scarcity mindset, he says. It's making space for more true living.

"The more you know, the less you need," said Chouinard on National Public Radio's "How I Built This."

An avid fly fisherman, Chouinard once decided to forego the thousands of available fly shapes, colors and patterns.

"I've limited myself to one type of fly for the past year, and I've caught more fish than I've ever caught in my life. You can replace the hundreds of thousands of fly options with knowledge and technique."

He continued: "The hardest thing in the world is to simplify your life because everything pulls you to be more and more complex. If we decide on a simpler life, it's not going to be an impoverished life. It's going to be really rich."

My nine-year-old received a new baseball uniform once. Like his brothers before him, he inscribed Philippians 4:13 on his hat: "I can do all things through Christ who gives me strength."

Many young believers refer to this verse in terms of hitting home runs and scoring last second shots.

But when the Apostle Paul wrote it, he was actually talking about being content in all situations, particularly hard ones.

Contentment is about perspective, the lens through which one views the world.

An old story goes that oil tycoon John D. Rockefeller was once asked by a reporter, "How much money is enough?"

He replied, "Just a little bit more."

Rockefeller likely didn't subscribe to this Greek proverb: "Nothing will content a man who is not content with little."

Throughout my childhood a plaque sat on a counter in my boyhood home. It read, "I asked God for all things that I might enjoy life. He gave me life that I might enjoy all things."

I haven't always remembered that secret to happiness, but I haven't forgotten it either.

37 A BIBLE BELT SURVIVAL GUIDE

Except for a single semester in college, I have never not lived in the Bible Belt. I've often lived for long stretches in what some people call the Bible Belt buckles: Nashville, Dallas and Abilene, Texas.

For the carpetbaggers among us, the Bible Belt is that swath of the religious South not easily understood by eastern blue bloods, western free spirits or pragmatic Midwesterners, though the latter likely relates the most.

The Bible Belt culture is frequently stereotyped in national entertainment and media circles.

It is even parodied within itself by folks – yes, folks – like Jon Acuff, editor of the Web site "Stuff Christians Like," and Christian comedians Tim Hawkins, Tripp Crosby and John Crist.

These satirists certainly differentiate between (A) making light of the idiosyncrasies of God's people and (B) making fun of God.

They would also likely point out that Jesus himself had his biggest field days with the religious people of his day.

The humorists might even agree with Churchill's line, "Democracy is the worst form of government except for all the others," by saying the church is the worst form of religious organizations except for all the others. Jesus gave his spirit to his body, after all.

But sometimes we maintain our sanity by laughing at ourselves, which is my intent with the following survival tips.

Tip 1: Whether your radio station is The Fish, The Rock, The Way, The River, K-LOVE or W-JOY, the same record labels seem to control the playlist. It includes the same five songs, and they all sound about the same. For artistic health, mix in some U2 and Tim McGraw.

Tip 2: You will go to church with someone who makes you want to bathe in the baptistery when you finish talking to him. Tape your favorite grace scriptures about grace to your shampoo bottle.

Tip 3: There will be more service opportunities than you have time or energy to fulfill. Boundaries will blur as guilt creeps in. A well-timed decline of a volunteer invitation may keep you from burning out in areas that matter more.

Tip 4: Small groups have many names: care groups, community groups, life groups, heart groups, D groups, Hebrews 10:25 groups. They all mean the same thing: Christianity is more relational, vulnerable and transparent than most of us would naturally prefer.

Tip 5: Whether your group is church-sanctioned or just a band of believers, intimate allies will keep Christianity relational, not just cultural. The church started around a campfire beside a fishing boat.

Tip 6: If you hire a plumber with a fish on his truck, he may not be any better at plumbing – or treat you any more honestly – than a plumber with a Harley sticker. As President Ronald Reagan said, "Trust but verify."

Tip 7 (having only 6 tips would have been evil): Author John Eldredge tells the story of a tour guide he had in Normandy, France, the site of the Allies' World War II D-Day invasion.

The dull docent demonstrated nonchalance not commensurate with the heroism that happened there.

"He had all of the facts, but none of the story," Eldredge observed.

For believers deep in the Bible Belt, may the same not be said of us.

38 MY FRIENDS ARE OLD

Someone once played a mean trick on me. He or she signed me up for a 40th birthday party invitation mailing list.

I never asked to be on this list and I was not anywhere near the top of The Hill, but the invites just kept pouring in.

Age forty is a special time, I suppose. Hair changes color and/or volume. Bodies contort in ways that resemble cartoon characters.

Before forty, kids think their dads can do anything.

One time the kids and I saw some boxing highlights on ESPN's Sportscenter.

My five-year-old son asked me, "Hey, Dad, are you going to sign up for boxing?" as if it was as easy as registering for pee-wee football.

Eventually, one's children have an epiphany:

"My dad is not a professional athlete, a traveling musician, a stuntman after all. He is actually a salesman, a manager, a report generator."

Around mid-life, friends and family gather to mourn the loss of coolness. They recount stories of collegiate feats and youthful pursuits.

They tell tales of times before gravity fully descended, when metabolisms ran day and night, and when cholesterol and ED only came up in health class, not in Golf Channel commercials.

As I mentioned, when I was placed on the 40th birthday party invitation mailing list, I was well shy of forty.

While some guys were barreling toward middle age, I was gliding into my prime.

Oh, sure, I was already spending a good bit of my days turning off lights, flushing commodes, bringing bikes in out of the rain and pulling recyclables out of the trash.

But it's not like I was falling asleep in movies or developing a taste for olives.

I was dominating my son's pee-wee football practice, for crying out loud. AND THERE BETTER BE NO CRYING OUT LOUD!!!

Never had a meaner man held a blocking dummy - until he felt something snap in his right knee one practice.

Growing old gracefully is a challenge. Some forego red meat, then all meat, then dairy, then gluten.

I'm not clear what gluten is, but I'm confident I'm already avoiding it.

Denial is another challenge. Men attempt to stiff arm Father Time and Rogaine their strength. Women think outside the Botox for ways to reverse wrinkles.

The surest ways to attractiveness at forty, fifty and beyond is joy in one's heart and character in one's bones. There's simply no powder, cream, foam or silicone shortcut to these things.

I'm not sure which comes first: the joy and character or the good decisions that lead to them. Regardless, they inspire an attractiveness that affects, and surpasses, physical appearance.

Despite my relative youthfulness, I attended all those Over the Hill parties. I couldn't let my friends forget where they came from.

39 OVER THE HILL, UNDER THE SEA

The week I turned forty, there was lots of Elvis Presley talk.

I was born a few days after Elvis died in 1977. My mother thinks it was a kingly coincidence. My kids do not. My wife is undecided.

Forty happened fast, but going over the hill is not as bad as I feared. It's not a mountain, after all. It's just a hill.

I still have hair, at least when viewed from the front. From the back, it's a different story.

Scientists call it male pattern baldness. My wife calls it a solar panel for a you-know-what machine.

Okay, my wife has never actually said such a thing. I saw the line on a t-shirt in New Orleans one time.

Changes to one's hair, including the aggressive protrusion of hair from inside of one's ears and nose, are among the bodily differences time inspires.

Just as bodies change with the decades, so do the questions about the road of life.

The first decade of life asks, "Are we there yet?" The teenage years scream, "What a ride!" The twenties announce, "I've arrived." The thirties, with its focus on kids and career, wonder, "Am I getting anywhere?"

Then, you get to the top of the proverbial hill and ask, "Do

I like the view?" Many people don't.

It is here that a fork appears.

Will I (a) grow disgruntled with how things have turned out and take an off-ramp, or (b) stay the course and finish what I started?

People find plenty of justifications for the exits they take. By mid-life, the drip, drip, drip of life can fill to neck level. Life has a way of not meeting expectations, and a fortieth birthday can pronounce the disappointments.

"Disappointment is how you know you're alive," a friend told me once at a college reunion. He credited the quote to his wife.

The mid-life crisis is usually not a calculated decision. It is a compulsive one, like a survival mechanism or an effort to remain viable.

We innately know at age forty that the ride down won't be smooth or gradual. "Getting old isn't for sissies," old-timers say between doctor visits.

Hopefully, the hilltop visit sharpens our focus on what's important.

Author Morgan Snyder (www.becomegoodsoil.com) says most people spend their thirties building kingdoms: families, businesses, careers, organizations, etc.

Instead, he spent his thirties attempting to accumulate wisdom from dozens of older, wiser men.

Snyder concluded that people are like icebergs: ninety per cent is below the surface. Behavior and actions above the surface only tell a fraction of the story. What lies beneath reveals the real motives.

The person who excavates his life and lays a firm foundation built on timeless wisdom – that is the person who can take the hill and keep on climbing.

40 DAD'S AGE IS A POPULAR PUNCHLINE

The older our kids get, the older they realize their dad is. He who began as an invincible specimen of heroism has ended up as a punchline of jokes.

As our kids grow, poking fun of my age is becoming a popular pastime.

"Want me to get that for you?" one of them asked as I stooped down to pick up an empty cardboard box.

"If you're being sincere, yes," I said. "Otherwise, no."

Some questions are more honest but no less insulting, such as when a seven-year-old asked, "Dad, what year were you born? Do you remember?"

Do I remember?!? I'm trying to forget!

I'm also starting to get a lot of history questions:

What year was the Final Four first played in a dome? How did people lose all their money during The Depression?

What do I look like, a walking Wikipedia? No, just a middle-aged man, someone who spends a majority of his days turning off lights and flushing commodes.

The kids have pointed out my bald spot for some time. Now they are pointing out my gray hairs.

Just when I think they're listening attentively to my wise words, they're actually examining my pigment status!

Even legitimate questions wind their way to a joke.

"Dad, what's your favorite radio station?" an eleven-year-old asked over a family dinner one night.

"I like 106.7 FM The Eagle," I replied. "It plays classic rock along with some good songs from the 80s and 90s."

"Isn't that all classic rock?" a fourteen-year-old inquired with a smirk. Jerk.

As I enter my fifth decade of life, not only am I having trouble remembering my own age, I'm also having a hard time telling other people's ages. I'll look at some people and honestly not be able to tell you if they're twenty-seven or forty-five.

Others must have the same problem. People I've known for years are looking right through me at the grocery store. I should probably start wearing a name tag.

All is not lost. Aging is a gift of perspective for those willing to be trained by it. Consider it an annuity of humility.

Aging is also the only way to wisdom. With every gray hair my kids identify, I remind them, "It doesn't mean I'm old. It just means I know something!"

A culture that glorifies youth, beauty and technological wizardry often foregoes a firm foundation on its way to a house of cards.

The longer I live in this un-restored world, the less I want aging to stop. Most of my desires will be met only at the coming restoration of all things.

As author John Eldredge writes in "All Things New," heaven is far from floating cherubs and perpetual church songs. It's a return to Eden.

King David writes about a great renewal in Psalm 103 (MSG):

He redeems you from hell - saves your life!
He crowns you with love and mercy - a paradise crown.
He wraps you in goodness - beauty eternal.
He renews your youth - you're always young in his presence.

Even at the Restoration, I'm sure my kids will still find a way to harass me. There will certainly be laughter in the ever after, after all!

41 DECLARING INDEPENDENCE

Patriotism is fundamental in our family. We attend Memorial Day services at the city cemetery. We welcome Air Force basic trainees into our home for Thanksgiving.

Many selfless men and women fought, suffered and died for the principles on which the United States was built.

For more than two centuries, patriots have taken up arms to defend freedom in this country. They were and are willing to fight for a cause greater than themselves. We try to honor them as best we can.

That doesn't mean we always get our American history right. Our seven-year-old once asked me, "Who wrote the National Anthem? Was it Babe Ruth?"

Another time as an eight-year-old, he was tasked with bringing something to school that represented our family heritage.

"Dad, what's something that represents our family?" he asked glancing across the kitchen at a large red container on the counter. "Ketchup?"

Ketchup is pretty all-American.

While historical perspective can be elusive, Lone Star State pride is not.

I once quizzed a nine-year-old on the presidential chain of

command.

"Who takes power if both the President and the Vice President pass away?" I inquired.

"The Governor of Texas?" he asked with an impressive level of certainty. Come and take it!

But we always try to honor the rabble rousers who mustered the courage to stand up to the most powerful and oppressive political power of their time.

The men who signed the Declaration of Independence put their names and lives on the line in historic fashion.

"About the Declaration there is a finality that is exceedingly restful," concluded President Calvin Coolidge on the 150th anniversary of the Declaration's signing.

Coolidge continued, "If all men are created equal, that is final. If they are endowed with inalienable rights, that is final. If governments derive their just powers from the consent of the governed, that is final. No advance, no progress can be made beyond these propositions. If anyone wishes to deny their truth … the only direction in which he can proceed historically is not forward, but backward."

Coolidge nailed it. In the Declaration of Independence, we fundamentally have it as good as it gets. The practice of government can always improve in a dynamic world, but the theory needs no change.

The beliefs laid out in the summer of 1776 can be summed this way: Government was made for people. People were not made for government.

A free people are not equal, and equal people are not free.

Colonial America saw an epic battle between freedom-loving people and an overreaching government.

The colonists wanted local government; King George wanted centralized authority. The colonists wanted limited taxation; George wanted to expand it. The colonists wanted more international trade; George wanted it stifled. The colonists wanted George's army and bureaucrats out of their homes and lives; George wanted refrigerator rights.

No wonder George had a fight on his hands.

In our time, nonviolent battles over government's proper role happen all around us. Why? Because the natural order in a fallen world is for power to expand and encroach.

May we not be unaware of or ill-prepared for the battles. May we not be so oblivious that we write in our diaries what King George wrote in his on July 4, 1776: "Nothing of importance this day."

42 BIG BENT ON ADVENTURE

After a hearty chicken fried steak in Fort Stockton, Texas, three friends and I entered Big Bend National Park for three nights in the backcountry.

We had high hopes for wildlife sightings. But by the end of day one, only ants, a lizard, some birds and a deer had crossed our path. At least we saw a 360-degree view of southwest Texas and northern Mexico from Emory Peak.

Day two began with a view, too. The "South Rim" overlooks the desert floor and the Rio Grande River 2,000 feet below.

It's a majestic collision of two nations. Grand mountains and deserts line both sides of a still grand river.

After hiking past a half dozen equally impressive overlooks, we arrived mid-afternoon at the same campsite where we had heard a mountain lion roar four years before.

With tempered expectations of a major wildlife sighting, we set up camp, soaked in the shade and looked around for signs of life.

The sun slowly descended along with our hopes. Then, as we chatted around an imaginary campfire – Big Bend is synonymous with burn bans – I spotted movement out of the corner of my eye.

Unaware of our presence, two 300-pound Mexican black

bears lumbered up the highland meadow.

For a few moments, nature mimicked art.

My comrades and I jumped up, half in self-defense, half to sightsee, not really knowing whether to grab a knife or a camera.

Our motion startled one bear thirty feet into a tree. The other hunkered down in the tall grass before making her way slowly up the opposite hillside.

After a few minutes, the bear in the tree climbed cautiously down and began sniffing for berries. From a distance of less than fifty feet, he grazed and watched us while we, amazed, watched him.

When I got home, I showed a video of the bear to my family.

"That's amazing!" said my three-year-old before turning to his mom, "Can we say 'amazing'?"

Yes, son, you can say amazing.

43 WHY WE LOVE CHIK-FIL-A

The announcement "Guess what, kids? We're having pizza tonight!" just doesn't garner the same response it did a generation ago.

In fact, I actually heard groans from the backseat the last time I uttered such a phrase. Those entitled little…

Our convenience-driven culture has made fast food more norm than exception.

But one stop always gets the kids' stamp of approval: Chik-fil-A.

When Chik-fil-A founder Truett Cathy opened his first restaurant in 1946, he and his brother rotated 12-hour shifts at the always-open diner.

Twenty-four hour dives were multiplying after World War II, and the brothers saw theirs as a way out of poverty.

The exhausting strings of twelve-hour days committed Cathy to a pillar of his future success: Closed Sundays. He needed the break.

Remembering the Sabbath has helped Chik-fil-A ascend to the largest grossing fast food chain in America. The company has about 2,000 stores in 46 states.

For many years, we went to church near a Chik-fil-A. The fact that we couldn't have it after Sunday worship made us want it all the more, the way not being able to enter your bank on Sunday makes you love your bank all the more. Sort of.

Sunday scarcity only scratches the surface of why we love Chik-fil-A. Here are other reasons:

1. Polynesian Sauce – I try not to think about the four sugar canes that go into each serving of the glazy condiment. I focus instead on how much my global worldview is expanding with every smothered bite.

2. Cows – Since first appearing on a Texas billboard in 1995, the Chik-fil-A cows have been the restaurant's official spokes-mammals. The world's most famous bovines warned us of the evils of red meat long before the World Health Organization.

3. Service – How can this person possibly be this excited to take my order? Probably because she just snuck a waffle fry.

Chik-fil-A's minimally-tattooed, maximally-spirited staff sets a standard of friendly service rivaled only by the People People at Southwest Airlines.

4. Innovation – The originator of the breaded chicken sandwich, Chik-fil-A keeps finding things that work.

They have great lemonade. They have great soft serve vanilla ice "dream" cones. Why not put them together for a Frosted Lemonade? They did.

And why not put two guys with iPads on the curb to take orders and payments faster. Last time I went, they did that, too.

5. Playground Purell – Ever attuned to the hopes and fears of soccer moms everywhere, Chik-fil-A provides sanitary wipes next to their indoor play areas. They also provide self-adhesive plastic mats to cover the tables in front of one-year-old "pinchers." Little things, big difference.

6. Food – It's delicious. It's not un-nutritious. It may be deep-fried, but it's also been immersed in instrumental worship music. Plus, pickles are cucumbers and cucumbers are vegetables. Green vegetables, for that matter.

7. Spirit – Maybe they're just located in areas where you do your Christmas shopping, but there's something transcendent about Chik-fil-A. Can I get an amen?

Chik-fil-A's drive-thrus are always filled with chunky SUVs.

Its dining rooms are always filled with chunky two-year-olds.

Orders are fulfilled accurately, unlike the time at a burger restaurant who shall remain nameless.

I placed a to-go order and asked for all the kids' burgers to be "ketchup only." When I got home, I realized they had taken me literally. There was no meat on any of the buns, only ketchup.

The experience brought new meaning to the phrase, "Where's the beef?" and it reminded me to EAT MOR CHIKIN.

44 THE MIRACLE THAT IS SOUTHWEST

A visit to extended family members outside of Texas put me on a Southwest Airlines flight one summer. The Dallas-based company still gives a breath of fresh air to otherwise tedious air travel.

Graduate business schools study Southwest for its human resources, corporate efficiency and customer service feats. "Hire for attitude and train from there." is their mantra as I remember it, and as I experience it.

Even as Southwest has acquired other airlines and added longer haul domestic and international flights, the company still seems to find enough "people people" to service its growth.

Permitting employees to be themselves while doing their jobs is risky business, but Southwest has reaped the rewards.

Rather than stuffing employees into corporate overhead bins, Southwest allows painting outside the lines. And this in a regulated industry that requires things inside the lines.

That paradox captures the brilliance of Southwest.

When post-September 11th rules and restrictions became more inane, mundane and insane, Southwest flight attendants turned them into fodder (while still getting messages across, of course.) They simply followed in the footsteps of their irreverent founder, Herb Kelleher.

Southwest made flying tolerable. The worse the Transportation Safety Administration treated you (remember "Don't touch my junk!"?), the more you wanted to fall softly into the outspread wings of Southwest.

"If you'll listen to these pre-flight instructions like it was your first time to hear them," a flight attendant said on my flight, "I'll pretend like it's my first time saying them."

"It's time to stow all electronic devices," she continued, "such as laptops, blenders and weed whackers." The mental image cracked me up.

She wasn't finished: "Please fasten your seatbelt like Beyoncé wears her pants: tight and low on the hips."

Even the pilot got in on the fun.

"The flight deck would like to welcome you to Flight 5602 with service to San Antonio and continuing service to New Orleans and Sydney, Australia."

Sydney? Southwest flies to Mexico and the Caribbean these days but not quite to the South Pacific.

When we landed, the pilot "accidentally" welcomed us to a random city far from our actual destination. I felt a shock spring up my spine.

"I'm sorry, folks," he said with a laugh. "It's my second day on the job." The line got lots of laughs, but only because we were already safe on the ground.

With booking and boarding systems so smooth, personnel so competent and prices so competitive, flyers tolerate Southwest's general admission seating and crowded cabins relatively void of creature comforts.

Southwest's mindset seems to be: "The pompous class can pay up somewhere else for a first class seat with personal TV screen. Those blue bloods won't get our jokes anyway."

A college friend has worked for Southwest for years. She recalls the time the airline offered $29 fares to select regional cities. The promotion was advertised on Monday Night Football.

First-time flyers came out of the woodwork. Their most popular form of luggage? Brown paper grocery sacks.

While Southwest is more than a common man's airline – yes, plenty of businesspeople refer to the airline as their "corporate jet" – you can bet Southwest's people people treated the flying football fans like owners of the team.

45 A REAL, LIVE CLARK GRISWOLD

Our annual search for festive Christmas light displays took us down an overlooked street in an older part of town.

108 Cedar Street is a regular rental house eight months out of the year. For three months it's a full-fledged construction zone, and for one month each December, it's every kid's Christmas night dream.

"Dad, it's for you. It's about the lights," Jimmy Sartain's daughter announced with a little bah-humbug. From the sound of things, she may not carry on the tradition passed down from Sartain's late father.

"I wasn't sure I was going to do the lights this year," Sartain said with a tear in his eye. His father had passed away earlier in the year.

"But when I told a neighbor that, you'd think I had just stepped on his baby chickens," he confessed.

Sartain did ground some attractions: a Santa-bearing helicopter and icicle strings that crossed over the road.

"Even still, small aircraft think my house is an airstrip," explained Sartain, who does electrical work at a local airfield.

Despite the scale-down, a Christmas train still chugs, a chimney still smokes, a holiday hot air balloon still inflates, lights still flash to Carol of the Bells or another of twenty-nine

Christmas tunes.

And a holographic Santa still speaks to your kids.

"The look on the kids' faces is priceless when they see him. Even parents do a double-take," Sartain said.

Here's Sartain's spectacle by the numbers:

100,000 lights

30,000 watts of electricity

1,500 visiting vehicles

92 electrical switches

9 miles of extension cord

6 Light-o-rama "brains"

1 computer

And the electric bill?

"It's kinda high," Sartain understated. "It was $1,500 three years ago. It'll probably be around $700 this year."

Hence the need for the donations box beside a string of candy canes Sartain put out for the kids.

"I've gotten about 60 bucks so far this year," he said.

And what do the neighbors say?

"They pretty much call me Griswold," referring to the cult classic character played by Chevy Chase in the 1989 comedy Christmas Vacation. Fittingly, an RV adorns the premises.

"That's Santa's cabin," Sartain explained. "It holds a lot of the switches."

To maintain relations with his neighbors, Sartain switches off the festivities by 9 p.m. on weeknights and 10 p.m. on weekends. He mows one neighbor's grass for the right to stretch his bright kingdom across her otherwise dark domain.

Sadly, some visitors aren't so neighborly. An empty space sits in a nativity scene where baby Jesus once laid.

"I heard some kids were having one of those scavenger hunts," Sartain said. "Somebody needed a baby Jesus, I guess."

Particularly somebody who steals one.

How does Sartain support himself and his high voltage habit? He's an electrician, of course. His father was a postman. That seems appropriate. The elder Sartain delivered kids' visions to Santa. His son delivers Santa's visions to kids.

When you turn into Sartain's self-contained neighborhood, a street sign will say "No Outlet." But don't believe it.

There are actually many outlets, all being put to very good use.

46 KIDS CAN'T NOT BELIEVE

Kids - at least my kids - just can't seem to do certain things.

They can't turn off a flashlight before setting it down. They can't put their shoes in the same place twice. And they can't forget even the slightest promise I make.

"But you said!" they remind me incessantly.

At Christmastime, I'm reminded of another thing kids can't do: They can't not believe.

Since the world is bigger than them, they assume there's a world beyond them. Hence, the magic of Christmas.

A few years ago, we introduced our kids to Elf on the Shelf.

We got the Spanish version, Una Tradición Navideña. The store was out of the English one. The language barrier wasn't a problem, however. The kids got the point.

For those farther behind than I, "The Elf on the Shelf" is a book that came out in 2005. It comes with an accompanying twelve-inch elf doll.

Once you read the book, the elf is supposed to appear in a different place in your house each morning. It helps Santa keep an eye on things.

According to the book, the elf technically flies to the North Pole each night and returns to a different spot the following morning. Kids love exploring the house looking for where it landed.

Our elf is a female named Valeria. She has shown up in glass cabinets, on ledges, in stockings and on Christmas tree branches.

Once, she appeared on a ceiling fan blade that got accidentally turned on. No human is supposed to touch the elf, so we carefully wrapped her in a towel and repositioned her in a stable place at a lower elevation.

If someone does touch the elf, The Elf on the Shelf web site gives recommendations to help your elf get its magic back: write an apology, sprinkle cinnamon or sing a carol with your family.

The web site also gives explanations for what might have happened if your elf returns from its overnight trip to the North Pole and lands in the same place it spent the prior day (a.k.a. your parents forgot to move it):

- It's the elf's favorite spot.

- The spot has a great view.

- The elf is preparing for a really special surprise the next day.

- The elf ate too many cookies at the North Pole and was too tired to move.

- The elf did move. Look closely! Work on your observation skills!

The web site makes no mention of a correlation between the elf's immobility and a parent's exhaustion level.

No matter the peculiarity of Valeria's movements, or lack thereof, my kids are still convinced of her magical powers.

I can't make them not believe any more than a grungy mall Santa can make them not believe.

Mark 9:23 captures a child's resilience to doubt: "Everything is possible for one who believes."

The Christmas story is full of the impossible made possible. Jesus, born to a young Jewish virgin, is the climax.

But there was another miraculous birth in the run-up to the incarnation: Jesus's relative John, born to Elizabeth, a barren woman.

The meaning for us is universal. Whether we're before our prime and scared, or past our prime and sad, the message is this: God is in the impossible. Believe!

47 HERDMANS, HERDSMEN AND ME

"What do you want for Christmas, Dad?" my six-year-old asked. "Maybe some dental floss?"

"Some what?" I replied, hoping I had misheard him. Surely he thinks I have more compelling Christmas wishes than floss!

Full disclosure: As a fifteen-year-old I requested a file cabinet from jolly old - and organized - Saint Nick.

To my chagrin, I had heard my son right. At least my hearing isn't going!

Woe is me. My offspring thinks I'm either mind-numbingly boring or that I have really bad teeth. Or worse, both.

Later that day, our family attended a classic heartwarming holiday play. It was the story of some hygiene-free rug rats who commandeer a church Christmas pageant.

Barbara Robinson's comedy "The Best Christmas Pageant Ever" has been a favorite of mine since I saw it performed in a community playhouse in the mid-1980s. It may have even sparked my love of redemption stories.

By way of review, the Herdman kids are a ragtag, uncouth, welfare-dependent bunch of bullies. Their parents are nowhere to be found. A social worker attempts to bring order to their chaos.

When the oldest child, Leroy Herdman, is tipped off that

Twinkies are served at the local Sunday School, the scraggly siblings suddenly find their religion. At Sunday School they hear about auditions for the church Christmas pageant.

After intimidating the buttoned-up church kids into relinquishing their starring roles, the Herdmans secure lead parts. Ralph becomes Joseph. Imogene plays Mary. Gladys gets her wings.

Church members are appalled.

"How could such riffraff be let into God's house to perform God's sacred nativity?"

"Mary and Joseph will look like poor travelers looking for a place to stay!" (Heaven forbid.)

"No one will come to the pageant!"

Wrong. Everyone came to the pageant – to see what the Herdmans would do. It was the most well-attended rendition in years.

The pageant unfolds as a story of redemption within a story of redemption. The Herdmans get swept up into the possibility that an all-powerful God just might care about them.

Magi Leroy Herdman offers the newborn king a canned ham straight out of the family's welfare box.

Angel Gladys Herdman announces Christ's arrival, "Hey! Unto you a child is born!" The story even broke through the hardened Imogene Herdman.

After the play concludes and the crowd disperses, Imogene returns alone to a darkened stage.

Overcome by emotion, she attempts to take in the events of the night, to treasure them in her heart. In tears, she clings to the swaddled savior of the world.

Imogene was as unlikely a carrier of the baby Jesus as Mary was herself. Therein lies the story's glory: God acting in the lives of ordinary people, the kind of people who get dental floss and file cabinets for Christmas.

Like the Herdmans on stage, the story of Christmas is equally unpredictable.

From virgin birth to shepherd witnesses to a daring midnight escape, nothing is as you or I would have drawn it up.

And how relieving is that? If a saving, gracing Creator can break through to Herdmans and herdsmen alike, just maybe he can break through to me.

48 WITH TEENAGERS, KEEP CALM AND PARENT ON

Interacting with a teenager is like dealing with a two-year-old in three ways.

First, he mainly communicates with grunts, groans, moans and noises.

Second, the fuller his tummy is, the less likely the conversation will end in a blowup.

Third, the more sleep he's gotten, the more likely you'll make it through without hearing "Why?" fifteen zillion times.

Still, somehow, he'll think you're the one asking too many questions.

"You ask too many questions," my teenager informed me in exasperation.

Evidently, my lone inquiry, "How are you doing?" put him over the top.

I understood. I used to cringe at questions from my folks.

Like him, I probably ended many conversations with a huffy, "May I be excused?" (teen speak for "I'm done talking.")

Nevertheless, I tried to explain to him that dialogue builds relationships.

Parents are, by nature, in the past. Trends come back in style because kids don't want to be like their outdated parents. My attire likely looks more like my grandfather's than my father's.

A piece of trivia came up at dinner recently: "A hotel was built in Hawaii in 1919."

"Wasn't that when you were born, Dad?" one son asked in a line of joking that - ironically - never gets old.

"No, he was born in 1914," another son chimed in.

The older I get, the more birthdays mean, and the more I want to embellish them.

Recently, my wife and I were planning a family birthday outing for our soon-to-be fifteen-year-old.

"Why?!?" the teenager asked, channeling his inner toddler.

"We want to celebrate with you," I said.

"I want to celebrate with my friends," he retorted in no uncertain terms.

Anyone who has lived with hormones knows they never stay constant. It wasn't much later that he backtracked,

"Well, maybe we can go out to dinner or something."

At that point his stomach was full and his frontal lobe was developed just enough to remember that he will get hungry again and he'll prefer a parent pay for his meal.

It's uncanny how much we all can turn, for the better, when we just let a little out. I'm not the same person after I do. He's not the same person after he does.

When teenagers are diffusing and refuting, it's important to keep calm and parent on, the Brits might say. Things only become a big deal when you make them a big deal.

Letting out a little rope also helps.

"How late did you stay up?" I asked when I picked him up the morning after a night at a friend's house.

"Guess," he invited.

"Five a.m." I conjectured.

With wide eyes he asked, "How did you know?"

"I was a teenager once," I explained. "I, too, had inquisitive parents."

Then, I became one.

I know he'll soon get annoyed again by questions from his

old man. I also know he would get more alarmed if I quit asking them.

49 LAST DARNDEST THINGS

When our oldest son was three, our preacher walked through the auditorium asking kids for their favorite Bible story. He raised his hand.

"The football player," he announced. I hope he was thinking about Goliath.

When our daughter was three, she invited me into a game of "I Spy."

"I spy something blue," she said.

"The sky?" I asked.

"No," she replied.

Her five-year-old brother overheard and chimed in: "The tree?"

"Yes!" she announced.

When she was five, she was attempting to improve both her spelling and her handwriting.

"Dad?" she asked. "How do you spell 'opportunity' in cursive?"

When you're five, the sky is the limit!

Speaking of sky, a seven-year-old son once gazed at a full moon behind some low-hanging, fast-moving clouds.

He yelled to his ten-year-old brother, "Hey! Come look at how fast the moon is moving!"

Like a seasoned scientist, the elder brother strutted over to clarify the natural phenomenon, "The moon's not moving," he said with a certain nonchalance. "We are."

He's definitely a logical thinker with an eye for detail. As a four-year-old he refused to eat watermelon because "it has peas in it."

He once saw a crescent moon and asked, "Is the moon broken?"

As a four-year-old he walked alone into a grove of trees. Later I asked him what he saw. His calm but snarly response: "Fierce animals."

I once asked him, "Who went tee-tee in the garage?" He instinctively passed the buck: "A skunk did."

We have other naturalists in the bunch. One diagnoses pathologies in animals from a distance.

"That squirrel is acting crazy! It probably has diabetes."

Another brother is mastering life cycles.

"At first it's a raccoon. Then it becomes a butterfly."

On a hike one time, this son asked, "Can butterflies kill us? What about ladybugs?" He's always been our most cautious kid.

His twin sister is more adventurous. She doesn't mind snakes, spiders or even "Venus fly swatters."

She has mastered bedtime delay tactics. After I explained that all of her brothers were asleep, she said, "You need to stay with me. I feel a bad dream coming on."

After some paternal soothing and insistence that she go to sleep, she bargained, "First, let me see your muscles."

She clearly knows how to push my buttons.

At Cracker Barrel, I beat her in a game of checkers. She didn't get mad, just even. "Daddy, give me your armpits. You get a tickle."

While I was improving my self-esteem at the checkers table, the other kids were exploring toys and trinkets in the country store.

"I wish I could live here!" announced a seven-year-old.

While he loves to build stuff, he doesn't like to waste time. On the way into Home Depot once, he said, "Dad, please don't stare at all the stuff you don't need."

Candy brings out the worst in us. One time, a twin had some; his sister didn't.

In tears, the have-not pleaded, "But you're supposed to share with me! We're twins, remember?"

Our definition of communal living often includes drinking from the jug and eating from the serving bowl.

After I instructed a seven-year-old not to eat from the ice cream carton, he rationalized, "I'm not. I'm eating from the spoon!"

When he dropped some of the sweet stuff and ants started swarming on the kitchen floor, he explained their existence, "Those are our pet ants."

I understand. To a red-blooded boy, there is very little difference between pest and pets.

In a houseful of boys, sibling rivalry raises its ugly head at times, like when your kids are playing an innocent game of "I spy" and then you hear, "I spy something ugly…"

When an eleven-year-old received a football award at a sports camp after throwing a touchdown pass to his younger brother, the nine-year-old said with a smile, "I should have dropped it."

"Who wants to play, 'Simon Says?'" an older brother asked one afternoon in the swimming pool. "I promise you won't make it past the first round."

"Yes, I will!" a little brother said enthusiastically.

The older brother started the game: "Simon says go underwater."

It's not just the boys who get in on the rivalries. Our little girl can apply her own dose of passive aggressiveness toward her older brothers.

During a campout with four other families, she organized a competition and asked for volunteers.

Knowing her gregarious ten-year-old brother wouldn't be able to resist raising his hand, and knowing he can't stand bananas, she coaxed him into coming up front.

Then, she announced the game: "It's a banana-eating contest!"

EPILOGUE: LONG DAYS, SHORT YEARS

As all parents know, these years, these quips and these memories fly by like a ball toward a window.

It is certainly hard to remember everything. I once told our kids the story of our first date. A nine-year-old then asked about our second and third dates.

"I don't remember exactly what we did," I replied honestly. "You'll need to ask your mother."

"She won't remember!" he exclaimed, a bit perturbed. "She can't even remember how old I am!"

Don't take it personally, son. We know you're heading in the right direction.

His little brother once captured how the whirlwind feels: "Mom, what was today? Yesterday?"

During these long days and short years, when five years feels like five seconds and the moments are sticky but they don't stick around for long, we'll do well to remember this prayer of Moses in Psalm 90:12:

"Teach us to number our days aright, that we may gain a heart of wisdom."

ABOUT THE AUTHOR

Kevin Thompson lives in the Texas hill country with his wife, Sarah, and their five school-aged kids. He formerly served as chief of staff for Texas Representative Dan Branch and has spent the last ten years writing a regular column in his local paper. He studied communication and ministry at Abilene Christian University before completing an MBA at The University of Texas at Austin. Thompson is now in commercial lending. He and Sarah have roots in Tennessee, but, like volunteers before them, they now fight for freedom in Texas.

Contact:
Kevin Thompson
kt@kevinwthompson.com
www.kevinwthompson.com

Made in the USA
Middletown, DE
29 April 2021

38149088R00087